QUICK AND EASY
INDIAN
MEALS IN MINUTES

Quick and Easy Indian Meals in Minutes

by

Thomas K. Neill

foulsham

LONDON · NEW YORK · TORONTO · SYDNEY

foulsham

The Publishing House, Bennetts Close,
Cippenham, Berkshire, SL1 5AP, England

Dedication

To my mother, brother and Yvonne

ISBN 0-572-02187-9

Cover photograph © Anthony Blake, Photo Libary

Printed in Great Britain by
Cox & Wyman Ltd, Reading, Berkshire

CONTENTS

INTRODUCTION

Most of the time we eat Indian food prepared in the conventional cookery-book way, often a time-consuming process. However rewarding it may be, we don't all have the time to devote to creating such meals. This book sets out to give you quicker alternatives which will give you the familiar taste of your favourite curries, with much of the hard work taken out.

I had my first taste of 'curry' from a scruffy little take-away in Manchester about 20 years ago, and ever since then I have liked Indian food and now and again wanted to re-create that taste of so many years ago. For a long time I tried but failed to reproduce at home those same smooth, tasty sauces. I tried liquidising the cooked sauces, in the hope that this was the answer to a smooth sauce ... it wasn't. I bought or consulted practically every Indian cookery book, but found that none of the recipes, however delicious, bore any resemblance to that first meal. I finally decided that take-aways obviously used some secret ingredient that couldn't be purchased outside the Indian restaurant or take-away trade.

At last I discovered that the way my neighbours, the Moughal family from Kashmir, cooked their sauces produced the texture and taste closest to the taste that I had been trying to achieve for so long. I have included their recipe in this book (page 26). I was surprised when I was shown how they made their basic 'curry' – they used commercial curry powder and added some spices. And most, but not all, of the spices they used were bought ready ground in small tins, a much quicker and simpler alternative.

It was another surprise to me that most of the ingredients for the curry were placed in a saucepan and boiled until the meat was tender, which was then removed. The sauce was rubbed through a sieve (strainer) and simmered until thickened. This produced a smooth, velvety sauce, smelling and tasting remarkably like the one I remembered from my first Indian meal.

The meat was cooked along with the onion in this recipe, but other recipes from the family varied. In some cases the meat was cooked separately in water with curry powder. In other recipes onions, oil, water and garlic were cooked until completely tender, then puréed and frozen to be used at a later date. This is the method I have used for a number of the recipes in this book.

Practically all the sauces made in the Moughal household used the same basic ingredients – onions, water, oil and garlic – and, to give variety, different spices and herbs were added, but in none of the sauce recipes was the onion ever fried first; it was always boiled then sieved.

The family had their own tandoor oven – an old chimney-pot in the garden – in which they cooked kebabs, tandoori chicken, naan bread, chapattis and so on. Everything tasted just as good as anything I had tasted from an authentic tandoor oven in a restaurant or take-away. I must admit I have always intended making my own tandoor in the same way, but have never got round to it. But I do all tandoor-type recipes successfully in the oven or under the grill.

Now you can make your own Indian food cheaply, quickly and easily at home and achieve excellent results. Especially if you are able to prepare some of the sauces or meats in advance, you will find that you can put together a delicious meal in very little time.

Most of the recipes in this book are based on my interpretation of the dishes available at Indian restaurants, and can be frozen so that you have a ready-made take-away to hand whenever you want. I have had to make some concessions to time in the style of the recipes, so some may not be authentic in the strict sense of the word, but they do bear a close resemblance to those recipes used by my Pakistani friends in their own homes. What exactly is authentic anyway? Every Indian family could claim that theirs is the way to make a particular dish.

When serving the food, try to provide dishes which complement each other as regards spiciness. There will be very little variety if all the food is highly spiced or extra hot. If you don't like hotness in your food, reduce the amount of chilli powder, or omit it altogether: if you like heat, increase the amount. Personally, I don't like my food very hot (I feel that the hotter the food, the less you are able to appreciate the flavour), so the amount of chilli powder used in the recipes is designed to give a dish of medium hotness.

Most of the recipes in the book use ground ginger and garlic powder. There is no particular reason for this, I just happen to like the flavour better than that of fresh garlic or fresh root ginger. If you prefer, use the same quantities of fresh garlic and ginger as is given for powdered to start with, then, as with the chilli powder, increase or decrease them to suit your own particular taste.

Suggestions for set menus are given at the back of the book.

All the recipes provide enough for two people: if you want to cook for four, simply double the measurements. I always make double the quantity of each recipe and freeze one portion; this way I can save time and build up a variety of two-portion meals in the freezer. If you prefer to cook each recipe when you want to eat it, then a supply of one of the basic curry sauces or Onion Purée kept in the freezer is ideal. If you freeze in foil containers, ready to reheat, you can even serve the meal straight from the containers, as you might do with a take-away. That way, you can save yourself some washing up – especially if you throw them away afterwards rather than cleaning them to use again.

The ingredients you will use are widely available in larger

supermarkets but they will cost considerably less from an Indian or Pakistani grocer or cash and carry.

All the recipes are very straightforward. Some of the curry sauces will need a little time simmering away, but you can make them in advance and in quantity and they need little or no attention while they are cooking – they are certainly worth it in the end.

Spices, Herbs & Flavourings

When buying spices buy little and often to ensure their freshness.

Below are the main spices and ingredients used in this book. You should be aware that different manufacturers, shops or supermarkets may use slightly different spellings, or even sometimes different names. Should you be unable to find any of them in your supermarket, try a trip to your nearest Indian or Pakistani grocer or cash and carry. If you really can't get a particular spice, you can always omit it or make a substitute ... you will simply get a slightly different but equally tasty finished dish.

Ground Spices

Aniseed
Chilli powder
Cinnamon
Cloves
Coriander (cilantro/dhania)
Cumin (jeera)
Fenugreek (methe)
Garam masala
Garlic powder
Ginger

Mustard powder
Nutmeg
Paprika
Black pepper
Coarse black pepper
Ground turmeric (haldi)

Whole Spices

Bay leaves
Black peppercorns
Carom seeds (ajowan)
Cinnamon bark
Cloves
Coriander (cilantro) seeds (dhania)
Cumin seeds (jeera)
Fennel seeds (soonf)
Fenugreek seeds (methe)
Green cardamom
Green chillies
Red chillies

Curry Pastes and Powders

Curry paste
Tandoori paste
Kofta powder
Korma powder
Madras powder
Tandoori powder
Tikka powder

Additional Ingredients

Most of these are available from supermarkets but try Indian
or Pakistani shops for the more unusual ingredients.

Asafoetida (hing)
Chapatti flour (ata)
Fresh coriander (cilantro/dhania)
Creamed coconut

Curry leaves (neem ki patia)
Dosa mix
Dried fenugreek (methe)
Red food colouring powder
Yellow food colouring powder
Ghee
Fresh root ginger
Gram flour
Dried mint
Bottled mint sauce
Pomegranate seeds (anardana)
Popadoms, plain and spiced
Basmati rice
Rosewater

Fresh Coriander (Cilantro)

Fresh coriander (cilantro/dhania) provides a unique flavour impossible to achieve with any alternative. If you are unable to buy it it is very easy to grow your own from mid-April:

Place John Innes No. 2 compost in a flowerpot (any size) to within 2.5 cm/1 in of the top. Smooth the surface. Take about 10 ml/2 tsp of coriander seeds, place in a plastic bag and crush lightly with a rolling pin. Sprinkle on top of the compost and cover lightly with a thin layer (about 1 cm/ $^1/_2$ in) of the compost. Water and leave to grow out of doors in a sunny spot.

The plants should be ready after 4-5 weeks. When fully grown pull out of the pot, remove and discard the stems and keep the leaves. You can use the leaves immediately, or place them in a plastic bag and freeze them.

Stagger planting in three or four pots for a continuous supply throughout June to September.

NOTES ON THE RECIPES

When following a recipe, use either imperial, metric or American: do not move from one to the other.

- All spoon measurements are level: 1 tsp = 5 ml; 1 tbsp = 15 ml.

- Eggs are medium size unless otherwise stated.

- Use any good quality light oil unless a specific oil is listed.

- All preparation and cooking times are approximate.

- Always wash and peel, if necessary, fresh produce before preparation.

- All recipes provide enough for two people: if you want to cook for four, simply double the quantities.

- All cooking times are approximate. You may like to cook the individual recipes for a longer or shorter period, depending on the heat used, the type of fuel, etc. I use a gas hob and have the heat on low to medium. If your sauce bubbles furiously the heat is too high: if it doesn't bubble at all it is too low. Trial and error will determine the level of heat best for you.

- Nearly all the recipes with sauce suggest using 5 tbsp of Basic Curry Sauce or of Onion Purée. This is equivalent to about 150 ml/^{1}/$_4$ pt/^{2}/$_3$ cup. Personal preference will dictate how much or how little sauce you want; if you want more, double the amount of Basic Curry Sauce or Onion Purée.

- If you like a thinner sauce, add extra water towards the end of cooking, when you will be best able to see its consistency. If you want it thicker, cook for a little longer until some of the liquid has evaporated.

BASIC RECIPES

I usually make a large quantity of Basic Curry Sauce (page 22) and freeze it in 75 ml/5 tbsp portions using containers such as cream cartons or small freezer bags. You can also freeze precooked meats or prepare curry powders in advance so that you can speed up the cooking process when you are ready for your curry and have little time. Of course, if you are really short of time, you can buy ready-made curry powders or pastes and use them instead.

CURRY POWDERS

By using different curry powders you can provide variety of flavour in the finished dishes. Of course, if you like the taste of a particular curry powder, you can stick to just that one. I would advise making only small quantities at a time as the flavour may diminish if stored too long. I store my home-made curry powders in glass honey jars in a dark cupboard. All the curry powders and tandoori and tikka powders below can also be bought ready-made.

BASIC CURRY POWDER

Makes about 150 g/5 oz/²/₃ cup	Metric	Imperial	American
Coriander (cilantro) seeds	45 ml	3 tbsp	3 tbsp
Cumin seeds	15 ml	1 tbsp	1 tbsp
Fennel seeds	15 ml	1 tbsp	1 tbsp
Curry leaves (optional)	12	12	12
Ground turmeric	15 ml	1 tbsp	1 tbsp
Garam masala	15 ml	1 tbsp	1 tbsp
Aniseed OR five-spice powder	5 ml	1 tsp	1 tsp
Chilli powder	5-15 ml	1-3 tsp	1-3 tsp
Garlic powder	15 ml	1 tbsp	1 tbsp

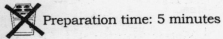

1. Put all the seeds and the leaves in a grinder and reduce to a fine powder.

2. Add the spices, mix together and store in an airtight jar.

Preparation time: 5 minutes

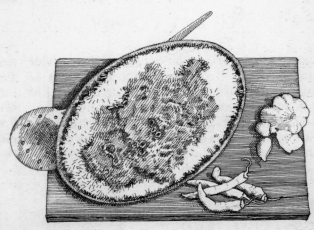

HOT CURRY POWDER

Makes about 150 g/5 oz/²/₃ cup	Metric	Imperial	American
Chilli powder	5-10 ml	1-2 tsp	1-2 tsp
Paprika	15 ml	1 tbsp	1 tbsp
Mustard powder	10 ml	2 tsp	2 tsp
Ground ginger	10 ml	2 tsp	2 tsp
Ground coriander (cilantro)	60 ml	4 tbsp	4 tbsp
Ground cumin	30 ml	2 tbsp	2 tbsp
Ground asafoetida	10 ml	2 tsp	2 tsp
Garlic powder	15 ml	1 tbsp	1 tbsp
Garam masala	15 ml	1 tbsp	1 tbsp

Mix together all the spices and store in an airtight jar.

 Preparation time: 5 minutes

MADRAS CURRY POWDER

Makes about 225 g/8 oz/2 cups	Metric	Imperial	American
Ground black pepper	15 ml	1 tbsp	1 tbsp
Chilli powder	15 ml	1 tbsp	1 tbsp
Mustard powder	10 ml	2 tsp	2 tsp
Ground ginger	15 ml	1 tbsp	1 tbsp
Ground turmeric	15 ml	1 tbsp	1 tbsp
Ground coriander (cilantro)	120 ml	8 tbsp	¹/₂ cup
Ground cumin	60 ml	4 tbsp	4 tbsp

Mix together all the spices and store in an airtight jar.

 Preparation time: 5 minutes

KORMA CURRY POWDER

Makes about 150 g/5 oz/²/₃ cup	Metric	Imperial	American
Ground turmeric	15 ml	1 tbsp	1 tbsp
Ground coriander (cilantro)	15 ml	1 tbsp	1 tbsp
Ground almonds	30 ml	2 tbsp	2 tbsp
Ground ginger	30 ml	2 tbsp	2 tbsp
Chilli powder	10-15 ml	2-3 tsp	2-3 tsp
Ground black pepper	5 ml	1 tsp	1 tsp
Ground cloves	5 ml	1 tsp	1 tsp
Ground cinnamon	10 ml	2 tsp	2 tsp

Mix together all the spices and store in an airtight jar.

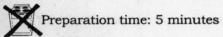 Preparation time: 5 minutes

MOUGHAL FAMILY CURRY POWDER

Makes about 150 g/5 oz/²/₃ cup	Metric	Imperial	American
Curry powder	45 ml	3 tbsp	3 tbsp
Paprika	45 ml	3 tbsp	3 tbsp
Ground turmeric	15 ml	1 tbsp	1 tbsp
Ground cumin	10 ml	2 tsp	2 tsp
Ground black pepper	10 ml	2 tsp	2 tsp
Ground coriander (cilantro)	5 ml	1 tsp	1 tsp
Chilli powder	10-20 ml	2-4 tsp	2-4 tsp

Mix together all the spices and store in an airtight jar.

Preparation time: 5 minutes

TANDOORI POWDER

Makes about 300 g/11 oz/2 ³/₄ cups	Metric	Imperial	American
Paprika	60 ml	4 tbsp	4 tbsp
Ground coriander (cilantro)	60 ml	4 tbsp	4 tbsp
Garlic powder	60 ml	4 tbsp	4 tbsp
Ground cumin	60 ml	4 tbsp	4 tbsp
Ground black pepper	5 ml	1 tsp	1 tsp
Red food colouring powder	5 ml	1 tsp	1 tsp
Dried mint	15 ml	1 tbsp	1 tbsp
Chilli powder	15 ml	1 tbsp	1 tbsp
Ground ginger	15 ml	1 tbsp	1 tbsp
Ground cinnamon	5 ml	1 tsp	1 tsp
Ground cardamom seeds	5 ml	1 tsp	1 tsp

Mix together all the ingredients and store in an airtight jar.

 Preparation time: 5 minutes

TIKKA POWDER

This quantity is enough to marinate 450 g / 1 lb of meat or chicken. See individual recipe on page 34.

Makes about 40 ml/2 ¹/₂ tbsp	Metric	Imperial	American
Ground coriander (cilantro)	15 ml	1 tbsp	1 tbsp
Ground turmeric	5 ml	1 tsp	1 tsp
Garlic powder	5 ml	1 tsp	1 tsp
Ground ginger	5 ml	1 tsp	1 tsp
Chilli powder	5 ml	1 tsp	1 tsp
Pinch of yellow food colouring powder			

Mix together all the ingredients and store in an airtight jar.

 Preparation time: 5 minutes

BASIC GARAM MASALA

Makes about 60 ml/4 tbsp	Metric	Imperial	American
Ground coriander (cilantro)	15 ml	1 tbsp	1 tbsp
Ground cinnamon	10 ml	2 tsp	2 tsp
Ground black pepper	5 ml	1 tsp	1 tsp
Whole cloves	10	10	10
Cardamom seeds	5 ml	1 tsp	1 tsp
Ground cumin	15 ml	1 tbsp	1 tbsp

Place all the ingredients in a grinder and reduce to a fine powder. Store in an airtight jar.

Preparation time: 5 minutes

FRAGRANT GARAM MASALA

Makes about 60 ml/4 tbsp	Metric	Imperial	American
Ground nutmeg	20 ml	4 tsp	4 tsp
Ground cloves	10 ml	2 tsp	2 tsp
Ground cinnamon	10 ml	2 tsp	2 tsp
Coriander (cilantro) seeds	20 ml	4 tsp	4 tsp

Place all the ingredients in a grinder and reduce to a fine powder. Store in an airtight jar.

Preparation time: 5 minutes

CURRY PASTE

Curry pastes are made of curry powder mixed with oil and vinegar (both of which give a longer storage life). If you don't want to buy commercial pastes, try the recipe below for your own curry paste.

Makes about 175 ml/6 fl oz/³/₄ cup	Metric	Imperial	American
Curry, tandoori OR tikka powder	50 g	2 oz	¹/₂ cup
Vinegar	50 ml	2 fl oz	3 ¹/₂ tbsp
Oil	50 ml	2 fl oz	3 ¹/₂ tbsp

1. Put the curry powder in a bowl and add the vinegar and just enough cold water to make a smooth paste about the consistency of unwhipped double (heavy) cream.

2. Heat the oil in a saucepan. Add the paste and stir for 10-20 minutes, until the water has evaporated. You should now have a thickish paste. Continue cooking gently until the oil separates. Allow to cool.

3. Place in clean warmed jars, cover tightly with the lids, and store until ready to use.

Preparation time: 5 minutes
Cooking time: 30 minutes

BASIC CURRY SAUCE

This is a good basic sauce if you want just a straightforward curry: add precooked meat, chicken or vegetables to it and heat through in the oven or on the hob. If you use the same curry powder each time, you will get a taste that never changes; vary the curry powders to get different tastes. They are delicious as they are, served with a biryani or rice dish.

Makes about 2.5 litres/ 4 ¹/₂ pts/11 cups	Metric	Imperial	American
For the spice base			
Curry powder	15 ml	1 tbsp	1 tbsp
Paprika	15 ml	1 tbsp	1 tbsp
Garam masala	15 ml	1 tbsp	1 tbsp
Ground turmeric	15 ml	1 tbsp	1 tbsp
Piece of cinnamon bark	5 cm	2 in	2 in
Canned tomatoes	200 g	7 oz	1 small tin
Tomato purée (paste)	15 ml	1 tbsp	1 tbsp
Salt	20 ml	4 tsp	4 tsp
Oil	150 ml	¹/₄ pt	¹/₂ cup
For the sauce base			
Garlic cloves	10 large	10 large	10 large
Root ginger, roughly chopped	25-50 g	1-2 oz	1-2 oz
Cold water	1.2 litres	2 pts	5 cups
Onions, peeled and roughly chopped	1.5 kg	3 lb	3 lb

1.   Put the first 4 spices in a cup and add 60 ml/4 tbsp of water. Stir well and set aside until required.

2.   For the sauce, liquidise the garlic and ginger with 150 ml/¹/₄ pt/²/₃ cup water, then place in a large saucepan with the other sauce base ingredients and the rest of the water and bring to the boil. Cover tightly and simmer for 45 minutes.

3. At the end of the cooking time, leave to cool, then liquidise or process until you have a completely smooth purée.

4. Return the purée to the pan and add all the spice base ingredients. Bring to the boil, then reduce heat and simmer uncovered for about 35 minutes, stirring from time to time.

 Preparation time: 10 minutes
Cooking time: 1 ¹/₂ hours

Basic Curry Paste Sauce

Follow the instructions for making Basic Curry Sauce, but omit the curry powder, paprika and tomato purée (paste) in that recipe and in their place add 1 jar (190 g) of bought or home-made curry paste at step 4, along with 10 ml/2 tsp of tomato purée (paste). This is interchangeable with the Basic Curry Sauce in the recipes.
   You can use the cleaned jars afterwards for storing your own home-made pastes.

Mild Curry Sauce

Heat a quantity of the Basic Curry Sauce, then stir in 10 ml/ 2 tsp of curry paste and 10 ml/2 tsp of tomato purée (paste). Leave to simmer gently until the sauce reaches the consistency you want. Finally, add 30 ml/2 tbsp of finely chopped coriander (cilantro) leaves.

ONION PURÉE

Some of the recipes in the book use just puréed onion, and not a Basic Curry Sauce.

Makes about 2.5 litres/ 4 ½ pts/11 cups	Metric	Imperial	American
Garlic cloves, peeled and chopped	10	10	10
Root ginger, roughly chopped	25-50 g	1-2 oz	1-2 oz
Onions, peeled and chopped	1.5 kg	3 lb	3 lb
Water	1.2 litres	2 pints	5 cups
Oil	120 ml	4 fl oz	½ cup

1. Liquidise the garlic and ginger with 150 ml/¼ pt/⅔ cup water, then place in a large saucepan with the other ingredients and bring to the boil. Cover tightly and simmer for 45 minutes.

2. At the end of the cooking time, leave to cool, then liquidise or process until you have a completely smooth purée.

3. Either use the puréed onion now or place in containers and freeze.

 Preparation time: 10 minutes
Cooking time: 50 minutes

Onion Curry Sauce

Stir 30 ml/2 tbsp of curry paste and 15 ml/1 tbsp of tomato purée (paste) into 150 ml/¼ pt/⅔ cup of Onion Purée and simmer until the sauce is the consistency you prefer. Finally, stir in 30 ml/2 tbsp of finely chopped coriander (cilantro) leaves.

PRECOOKED MEAT

I have used the Moughal method for preparing precooked lamb, beef or chicken (page 8).

I generally freeze in two-person portions of approximately 225 g/8 oz. If using chicken breast you can precook it or, as the cooking time is so short, you can use fresh. Chicken portions should be precooked as below, and can be used in place of chicken breasts in nearly all the recipes.

1.   For each 450 g/1 lb of meat cut into 2.5 cm/1 in cubes add 15 ml/1 tbsp of curry powder of your choice, 2 crushed garlic cloves (or 10 ml/2 tsp of garlic powder) and 1.2 litres/2 pts/5 cups of water.

2.   Place all the ingredients in a pan, bring to the boil and simmer until the meat is tender. Remove the meat and let it go cold.

Precooked Prawns (Shrimp)

You should allow approximately 225 g/8 oz for two people, of whichever type you like from small prawns to king prawns. Fresh prawns should be cooked just until they turn pink; do not overcook them. Thaw frozen prawns before use; they simply need to be warmed through.

Precooked Vegetables

Put 225 g/8 oz of vegetables of your choice in a pan with 600 ml/1 pt/2 $^1/_2$ cups of water and 5 ml/1 tsp of curry powder and cook until the vegetables are just tender. Drain.

THE MOUGHAL CURRY

This recipe, or a variation of it, is the basis for nearly all the
other curry recipes in the book and makes a very tasty curry.
It is reproduced below exactly as given to me.

Serves 4	Metric	Imperial	American
Meat, cut into 2.5 cm/1 in cubes	450 g	1 lb	1 lb
Onion, chopped	225 g	8 oz	2 cups
Garlic cloves, chopped	6	6	6
Tomato, chopped	1	1	1
Salt to taste			
Moughal Family Curry Powder (page 18)	30 ml	2 tbsp	2 tbsp
Tomato purée (paste)	15 ml	1 tbsp	1 tbsp
Water	900 ml	1 1/2 pts	3 3/4 cups
Oil	90 ml	6 tbsp	6 tbsp
Finely chopped coriander (cilantro) leaves	30 ml	2 tbsp	2 tbsp
Green chilli, chopped	1	1	1
Sugar	10 ml	2 tsp	2 tsp

1. Place the meat, onion, garlic, tomato, salt, curry powder,
    tomato purée and water in a large pan and boil for
    about 30 minutes until the meat is tender.

2. Remove the meat. Simmer the sauce until a piece of the
    onion can easily be crushed against the side of the pan
    with a spoon. Remove from the heat and cool a little,
    then rub the onion through a sieve (strainer) with a
    metal spoon.

3. Return the sieved sauce to the pan, add the oil and cook gently until the oil floats to the top and the sauce thickens slightly. Return the meat to the pan, add the coriander, chilli and sugar and simmer for about 5 minutes. If you like your sauce very thin, add more water: if you like it thicker, cook for a longer time.

Preparation time: 10 minutes
Cooking time: 45 minutes

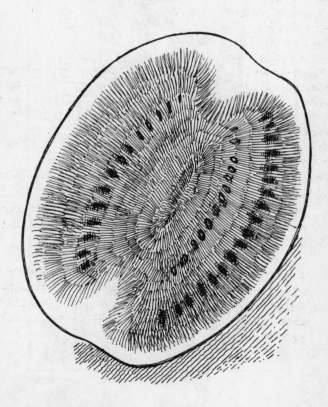

STARTERS

Here are some of my favourite Indian starters. You can serve them to whet the appetite for the main course – in which case keep the quantities fairly small or you will spoil your appetite rather than enhance it – or you can add some side dishes and use the recipes as a meal in their own right.

TANDOORI CHICKEN

Chicken marinated in yoghurt, herbs and spices.

Serves 4	Metric	Imperial	American
Chicken breasts (about 450 g/1 lb total weight)	4	4	4
For the marinade			
Natural (plain) yoghurt	150 ml	1/4 pt	2/3 cup
Garlic powder	5 ml	1 tsp	1 tsp
Ground cinnamon	10 ml	2 tsp	2 tsp
Tandoori Powder (page 19)	30 ml	2 tbsp	2 tbsp
Salt	10 ml	2 tsp	2 tsp
Curry paste or powder	15 ml	1 tbsp	1 tbsp
Ground coriander (cilantro)	5 ml	1 tsp	1 tsp
Chopped coriander (cilantro) leaves	60 ml	4 tbsp	4 tbsp
Garam masala	10 ml	2 tsp	2 tsp
Bottled mint sauce	5 ml	1 tsp	1 tsp
Lemon juice	15 ml	1 tbsp	1 tbsp

1. Slash the chicken breasts three or four times along their length (about 5 mm/^{1}/$_4$ in deep) to allow the marinade to penetrate the flesh.

2. Mix together all the marinade ingredients in a glass bowl. Add the chicken breasts and coat well, using your hands. Cover and marinate for several hours or preferably overnight in the fridge.

3. When ready to cook, preheat the oven to 190°C/ 375°F/gas mark 5. Place the chicken breasts on metal skewers and then on a baking tray. (You can cook the meat directly on a baking tray if you don't have skewers.)

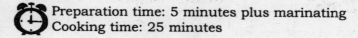

4. Cook for approximately 20-25 minutes, turning once after about 10 minutes.

5. Serve with Lemon Salad (page 141) or some sliced tomato and lemon wedges.

Preparation time: 5 minutes plus marinating
Cooking time: 25 minutes

TANDOORI KING PRAWNS

Prawns marinated in yoghurt and spices.

Serves 2	Metric	Imperial	American
King prawns (jumbo shrimp)	225 g	8 oz	¹/₂ lb
Lemon juice	45 ml	3 tbsp	3 tbsp
For the marinade			
Natural (plain) yoghurt	45 ml	3 tbsp	3 tbsp
Pinch of garlic powder			
Ground ginger	5 ml	1 tsp	1 tsp
Pinch of ground black pepper			
Pinch of chilli powder			
Curry paste	10 ml	2 tsp	2 tsp
Finely chopped coriander (cilantro) leaves	30 ml	2 tbsp	2 tbsp
Bottled mint sauce	5 ml	1 tsp	1 tsp
Tandoori Powder (page 19)	15 ml	1 tbsp	1 tbsp
Salt	5 ml	1 tsp	1 tsp

1. Put the prawns in a glass bowl and pour the lemon juice over. Leave for about 10 minutes.

2. Mix together all the marinade ingredients in a glass bowl. Add the prawns and coat well, using your hands. Cover and marinate for several hours or preferably overnight in the fridge.

3. When ready to cook, preheat the grill (broiler). Thread the king prawns on to skewers and cook for about 15 minutes, turning once or twice.

 Preparation time: 5 minutes plus marinating
Cooking time: 25 minutes

LAMB TIKKA

Lamb marinated in yoghurt and spices.

Serves 2	Metric	Imperial	American
Lamb, cubed	225 g	8 oz	1/2 lb
Lemon juice	25 ml	1 1/2 tbsp	1 1/2 tbsp
For the marinade			
Natural (plain) yoghurt	75 ml	5 tbsp	5 tbsp
Tikka Powder (page 19)	1/2 recipe	1/2 recipe	1/2 recipe
Salt	5 ml	1 tsp	1 tsp
Oil	30 ml	2 tbsp	2 tbsp

1. Put the lamb in a glass bowl and pour the lemon juice over. Leave while making up the marinade.

2. Mix together all the marinade ingredients in a glass bowl. Add the lamb and coat well, using your hands. Cover and marinate for several hours or preferably overnight in the fridge.

3. When ready to cook, preheat the grill (broiler). Thread the lamb cubes on to metal skewers and place on a baking tray. Grill (broil) for 20-25 minutes, turning often. Avoid cooking too fiercely or the lamb will be burned on the outside and raw in the middle.

4. Serve with Lemon Salad (page 141) and lemon wedges.

Preparation time: 5 minutes plus marinating
Cooking time: 25 minutes

CHICKEN TIKKA

Chicken marinated in yoghurt and spices.

Serves 2	Metric	Imperial	American
Chicken breast	225 g	8 oz	¹/₂ lb
Lemon juice	30 ml	2 tbsp	2 tbsp
For the marinade			
Natural (plain) yoghurt	75 ml	5 tbsp	5 tbsp
Tikka Powder (page 19)	¹/₂ recipe	¹/₂ recipe	¹/₂ recipe
Oil	15 ml	1 tbsp	1 tbsp
Salt	2.5 ml	¹/₂ tsp	¹/₂ tsp
Finely chopped coriander (cilantro) leaves	10 ml	2 tsp	2 tsp

1. Cut the chicken into 2.5 cm/1 in cubes and put in a glass bowl. Pour the lemon juice over. Leave while making up the marinade.

2. Mix together all the marinade ingredients in a glass bowl. Add the chicken and coat well, using your hands. Cover and marinate for several hours or preferably overnight in the fridge.

3. When ready to cook, preheat the oven to 190°C/375°F/ gas mark 5. Thread the chicken cubes on to metal skewers. Place in the oven on a baking tray and cook for 20-25 minutes, turning once or twice.

4. Serve with Lemon Salad (page 141) and lemon wedges.

Preparation time: 5 minutes plus marinating
Cooking time: 25 minutes

FISH TIKKA

Cod marinated in spices. Use the same recipe for king prawns (shrimp).

Serves 2	Metric	Imperial	American
Cod	225 g	8 oz	1/2 lb
Lemon juice	30 ml	2 tbsp	2 tbsp
For the marinade			
Natural (plain) yoghurt	75ml	5 tbsp	5 tbsp
Tikka Powder (page 19)	1/2 recipe	1/2 recipe	1/2 recipe
Pinch of ground ginger			
Oil	15 ml	1 tbsp	1 tbsp
Salt	2.5 ml	1/2 tsp	1/2 tsp
Finely chopped coriander (cilantro) leaves	30 ml	2 tbsp	2 tbsp

1. Cut the cod into 2.5 cm / 1 in cubes and put in a glass bowl. Pour the lemon juice over and leave while making up the marinade.

2. Mix together all the marinade ingredients in a glass bowl. Add the fish and coat well, using your hands. Cover and marinate for several hours or preferably overnight in the fridge.

3. Preheat the oven to 190°C/375°F/gas mark 5. Thread the fish cubes on to metal skewers and place them in the oven on a baking tray. Cook for 10-15 minutes, turning once or twice.

4. Serve with Lemon Salad (page 141) and lemon wedges.

Preparation time: 5 minutes plus marinating
Cooking time: 25 minutes

SHEEK KEBAB

Pungently spiced minced meat kebab.

Serves 2-4	Metric	Imperial	American
Ground coriander (cilantro)	5 ml	1 tsp	1 tsp
Ground ginger	5 ml	1 tsp	1 tsp
Ground turmeric	5 ml	1 tsp	1 tsp
Chilli powder	5 ml	1 tsp	1 tsp
Dried mint	5 ml	1 tsp	1 tsp
Large pinch of red food colouring powder			
Garam masala	5 ml	1 tsp	1 tsp
Tandoori Powder (page 19)	10 ml	2 tsp	2 tsp
Minced (ground) lamb OR beef	450 g	1 lb	2 cups
Finely chopped coriander (cilantro) leaves	45 ml	3 tbsp	3 tbsp
Salt	5-10 ml	1-2 tsp	1-2 tsp

1. Put the coriander, ginger, turmeric, chilli powder, mint, food colouring, garam masala and tandoori powder in a cup and mix to a paste with 45 ml/3 tbsp of water.

2. Put the minced lamb in a bowl, along with the chopped coriander, salt and spice mix from the cup, and knead everything together well with your hands, or process in a food processor for 15-20 seconds.

3. Cover the mixture and leave in the fridge for 2-3 hours for the flavours to develop.

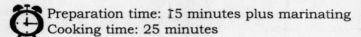

4. When ready to cook, preheat the oven to 190°C/375°F/ gas mark 5. Divide the mixture into 12 pieces and form each piece into a sausage shape. Thread three on to each of four skewers and place on a baking tray lined with foil. Cook for approximately 20 minutes, turning once half way through cooking.

5. Serve with Lemon Salad (page 141), Yoghurt and Mint Sauce (page 139) and Puri (page 135).

Preparation time: 15 minutes plus marinating
Cooking time: 25 minutes

MILD SHAMI KEBAB

Mild minced meat kebab.

Serves 2	Metric	Imperial	American
Minced (ground) lamb OR beef	225 g	8 oz	1 cup
Finely chopped onion	50 g	2 oz	1/2 cup
Small potato, grated	1	1	1
Green chilli, chopped	1	1	1
Chilli powder	5 ml	1 tsp	1 tsp
Garam masala	10 ml	2 tsp	2 tsp
Ground coriander (cilantro)	5 ml	1 tsp	1 tsp
Ground cumin	5 ml	1 tsp	1 tsp
Salt	5 ml	1 tsp	1 tsp
Gram flour	25 g	1 oz	1/4 cup
Oil for deep frying			

1. Mix together all the ingredients except the oil and knead well with your hands for about 2 minutes. With wet hands, form into rissoles about 7.5 cm/3 in across.

2. Deep fry for about 2 minutes until reddish-brown.

3. Serve with lemon wedges, a few slices of raw onion, Yoghurt and Mint Sauce (page 139) and Chapattis (page 135).

Preparation time: 10 minutes
Cooking time: 5 minutes

SPICY SHAMI KEBAB

Medium-hot minced meat kebab.

Serves 2	Metric	Imperial	American
Pomegranate seeds	10 ml	2 tsp	2 tsp
Coriander (cilantro) seeds	10 ml	2 tsp	2 tsp
Minced (ground) lamb OR			
beef	225 g	8 oz	1 cup
Ground ginger	5 ml	1 tsp	1 tsp
Finely chopped onion	50 g	2 oz	1/2 cup
Finely chopped tomato	25 g	1 oz	1/4 cup
Gram flour	25 g	1 oz	1/4 cup
Salt	5 ml	1 tsp	1 tsp
Chilli powder	5 ml	1 tsp	1 tsp
Pinch of carom seeds			
Ground cumin	2.5 ml	1/2 tsp	1/2 tsp
Finely chopped coriander			
(cilantro) leaves	45 ml	3 tbsp	3 tbsp
Oil for deep frying			

1. Grind the pomegranate and coriander seeds together and mix with all the remaining ingredients except the oil. Knead well with your hands for 2 minutes. With wet hands, form into rissoles about 7.5 cm/3 in across.

2. Deep fry for about 2 minutes until reddish-brown.

3. Serve with Lemon Salad (page 141), lemon wedges and Chapattis (page 135).

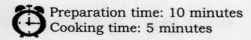 Preparation time: 10 minutes
Cooking time: 5 minutes

KEEMA SAMOSAS

Deep-fried pastries filled with spiced meat.

Serves 4	Metric	Imperial	American
For the filling			
Potatoes, peeled and cut into small dice	2 large	2 large	2 large
Chilli powder	5 ml	1 tsp	1 tsp
Dried mint	5 ml	1 tsp	1 tsp
Garam masala	5 ml	1 tsp	1 tsp
Garlic powder	5 ml	1 tsp	1 tsp
Ground ginger	5 ml	1 tsp	1 tsp
Oil	30 ml	2 tbsp	2 tbsp
Whole cumin seeds	5 ml	1 tsp	1 tsp
Onion, finely chopped	1	1	1
Minced (ground) lamb OR beef	110 g	4 oz	$^1/_2$ cup
Curry paste	10 ml	2 tsp	2 tsp
Pomegranate seeds	5 ml	1 tsp	1 tsp
Coriander (cilantro) seeds, roughly crushed	5 ml	1 tsp	1 tsp
Finely chopped coriander (cilantro) leaves	30 ml	2 tbsp	2 tbsp
Salt	10 ml	2 tsp	2 tsp
For the pastry			
Ghee OR butter	50 g	2 oz	$^1/_4$ cup
Plain (all-purpose) flour	225 g	8 oz	2 cups
Salt	5 ml	1 tsp	1 tsp
Hot water	85-120 ml	3-4 fl oz	5 $^1/_2$-7 tbsp
Oil for deep frying			

1. To make the filling, put the diced potatoes in a saucepan, cover with water and cook until just tender. Drain and set aside.

2. Put the chilli powder, mint, garam masala, garlic powder and ginger in a cup with 45 ml/3 tbsp of water. Set aside.

3. Heat the oil in a pan, and add the cumin seeds. Fry for about 30 seconds. Add the onion and fry until golden brown.

4. Add the mince and fry until browned.

5. Add the spice mix from the cup, and the curry paste along with the pomegranate and coriander seeds. Add the potato, coriander leaves and salt. Mix well then leave to go completely cold.

6. To make the pastry, rub the fat into the flour until it resembles fine breadcrumbs. Add the salt and mix to a stiffish dough with the hot water. Chill in the fridge.

7. Divide the pastry into eight and roll each piece on a lightly floured surface into as thin a circle as possible. (The thinner the pastry the crisper it will be when fried.)

8. Heat a frying pan until hot, then place each pastry circle in the pan and cook for no more than 5-10 seconds on each side. Remove from the pan and cut each circle in half.

9. Make a thickish paste in a cup with about 10 ml/2 tsp of flour and 5 ml/1 tsp of water. Take one of the half-circles and brush some flour paste along the straight edge. Now form the half-circle into a cone shape and put in about 2 tsp of the cold filling. Brush the top inside edge with the flour paste and press tightly together. Repeat with the remaining samosas.

10. Deep fry the samosas three at a time for about 4-5 minutes until golden. Make sure the heat is not too high.

 Preparation time: 10 minutes plus chilling
Cooking time: 30 minutes

Vegetable Samosas

Deep-fried pastries filled with spiced vegetables.

Follow the recipe for Keema Samosas (page 40) but replace the mince with 4 oz of chopped mixed vegetables.

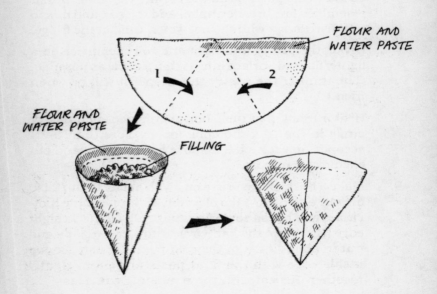

VEGETABLE PAKORA

Deep-fried spiced vegetables.

Serves 4	Metric	Imperial	American
Pomegranate seeds	15 ml	1 tbsp	1 tbsp
Coriander (cilantro) seeds	15 ml	1 tbsp	1 tbsp
Thinly sliced onion	225 g	8 oz	2 cups
Canned tomatoes, chopped	3-4	3-4	3-4
Potatoes, grated	450 g	1 lb	1 lb
Egg, beaten	1	1	1
Finely chopped coriander (cilantro) leaves	50 g	2 oz	2 oz
Green chillies, finely chopped	7	7	7
Green (bell) pepper, finely chopped	1 small	1 small	1 small
Chilli powder	15 ml	1 tbsp	1 tbsp
Gram flour OR plain (all-purpose) flour	350 g	12 oz	3 cups
Oil for deep frying			

1. Crush the pomegranate and coriander seeds roughly.

2. Put all the ingredients in a large bowl and mix well by hand. If the mixture is very dry add 15-30 ml/ 1-2 tbsp of water. Heat the oil for deep frying.

3. Take heaped teaspoonfuls of the mixture and drop gently into the hot oil. Cook for about 3 minutes until golden.

4. Serve with Lemon Salad (page 141), Yoghurt and Mustard Sauce (page 139) and Ginger and Date Chutney (page 140).

Preparation time: 10 minutes
Cooking time: 5 minutes

Chicken Pakora

Deep-fried spiced chicken.

Follow the recipe for Vegetable Pakora (page 43) but add 100 g/4 oz of chopped precooked chicken breast to the mixture.

Keema Pakora

Deep-fried spiced minced meat.

Follow the recipe for Vegetable Pakora but add 100 g/4 oz/ $1/2$ cup fried and drained minced (ground) lamb or beef to the mixture.

Make a large batch of pakora for freezing. Heat in the oven wrapped in foil, or microwave on reheat.

POTATO PAKORA

Deep-fried spiced potato.

Serves 2	Metric	Imperial	American
Potatoes	1-2	1-2	1-2
Gram flour OR plain (all-purpose) flour	100 g	4 oz	1 cup
Large pinch of chilli powder			
Large pinch of ground cumin			
Large pinch of ground turmeric			
Salt	5 ml	1 tsp	1 tsp
Oil for deep frying			

1. Peel and cut the potatoes into 5 mm / ¼ in thick slices.

2. Put the flour, spices and salt in a bowl. Add enough water to make a batter thick enough to coat the potato, just a little thicker than double (heavy) cream.

3. Heat the oil for deep frying.

4. Dip the potato slices in the batter and then fry them gently in the hot oil for 3-4 minutes until cooked through and golden.

5. Serve with Ginger and Date Chutney (page 140).

Preparation time: 10 minutes
Cooking time: 5 minutes

CURRY DISHES

Curry dishes can be freshly made with raw or cooked meats, fish or vegetables, or they are even quicker to put together if you have some curry sauce in the freezer. It's also a good idea to make a large quantity while you are cooking so that you can freeze finished dishes which can be ready to eat in an instant when you have no time at all.

CHICKEN DOPIAZA

Dopiaza dishes are very rich curries with fried onion.

Serves 2	Metric	Imperial	American
Chicken breast	225 g	8 oz	1/2 lb
For the sauce			
Oil	30 ml	2 tbsp	2 tbsp
Thinly sliced onion	175 g	6 oz	1 1/2 cups
Garlic powder	10 ml	2 tsp	2 tsp
Chilli powder	5 ml	1 tsp	1 tsp
Salt	5 ml	1 tsp	1 tsp
Sugar	5 ml	1 tsp	1 tsp
Finely chopped coriander (cilantro) leaves	30 ml	2 tbsp	2 tbsp
Basic Curry Sauce (page 22)	75 ml	5 tbsp	5 tbsp

1. Cut the chicken into 8-10 pieces.

2. Heat the oil and fry (sauté) the onion until golden brown. Remove to a plate, leaving the oil in the pan.

3. Add the chicken and stir-fry for about 7 minutes or until cooked.

4. Mix the garlic powder and chilli powder with 15 ml/ 1 tbsp of water in a cup.

5. Add the spice mix from the cup along with the salt, sugar and Basic Curry Sauce and cook for about 5 minutes until the sauce has reduced slightly. Stir in the coriander leaves and onion and heat through.

Preparation time: 5 minutes
Cooking time: 25 minutes

Lamb Dopiaza

Follow the recipe for Chicken Dopiaza but substitute 225 g/
8 oz of precooked lamb for the chicken at step 3, and cook
for 3 minutes instead of 7.

Keema Dopiaza

Follow the recipe for Chicken Dopiaza but substitute 225 g/
8 oz/1 cup of raw minced (ground) beef for the chicken at
step 3.

Prawn Dopiaza

Follow the recipe for Chicken Dopiaza but substitute 225 g/
8 oz of prawns (shrimp) or king prawns for the chicken at
step 3. Omit step 4. Omit the spice mix at step 5.

CHICKEN ROGAN JOSH

The flavour of these medium hot Rogan Josh dishes is obtained from tomatoes, peppers, fried onions and spices.

Serves 2	Metric	Imperial	American
Chicken breast	225 g	8 oz	1/2 lb
For the sauce			
Oil	30 ml	2 tbsp	2 tbsp
Finely chopped onion	175 g	6 oz	1 1/2 cups
Piece of cinnamon bark	2.5 cm	1 in	1 in
Whole cloves	3	3	3
Whole green cardamoms	3	3	3
Onion Purée (page 24)	75 ml	5 tbsp	5 tbsp
Tomato purée (paste)	15 ml	1 tbsp	1 tbsp
Green chillies, chopped	2	2	2
Finely chopped green (bell) pepper	50 g	2 oz	1/2 cup
Coarsely ground black pepper	10 ml	2 tsp	2 tsp
Garlic powder	10 ml	2 tsp	2 tsp
Sugar	5 ml	1 tsp	1 tsp
Salt	5 ml	1 tsp	1 tsp
Natural (plain) yoghurt	30 ml	2 tbsp	2 tbsp
Chopped tomato	100 g	4 oz	1/2 cup
Finely chopped coriander (cilantro) leaves	15 ml	1 tbsp	1 tbsp

1.   Cut the chicken into 8-12 pieces.

2.   Heat the oil and fry (sauté) the onions until golden brown.

3.   Add the chicken, cinnamon bark, cloves and cardamoms and cook until tender for about 7 minutes.

4.   Add the Onion Purée and cook for 2 minutes until reduced slightly.

5.   Add the tomato purée, chillies, green pepper, black pepper, garlic powder, sugar and salt and stir-fry for 2-3 minutes.

6.   Add the yoghurt and stir-fry for about 1 minute.

7.   Finally, add the chopped tomato and coriander leaves and heat through for about 2 minutes.

Preparation time: 10 minutes
Cooking time: 25 minutes

Lamb Rogan Josh

Follow the recipe for Chicken Rogan Josh but substitute 225 g/8 oz of precooked lamb for the chicken at step 3 and cook for only 4 minutes instead of 7 minutes.

Keema Rogan Josh

Follow the recipe for Chicken Rogan Josh but substitute 225 g/8 oz/1 cup of raw minced (ground) beef for the chicken at step 3.

Prawn Rogan Josh

Follow the recipe for Chicken Rogan Josh but substitute 225 g/8 oz/1 cup of prawns (shrimp) or king prawns for the chicken at step 3 and cook for only 1 minute instead of 7 minutes.

CHICKEN DHANSAK

Dhansak dishes use spices, lentils, pineapple and mixed vegetables combined to produce a sweet and sour flavour.

Serves 2	Metric	Imperial	American
Chicken breast	225 g	8 oz	1/2 lb
For the sauce			
Canned red or yellow lentils	45 ml	3 tbsp	3 tbsp
Oil	30 ml	2 tbsp	2 tbsp
Basic Curry Sauce (page 22)	75 ml	5 tbsp	5 tbsp
Canned ratatouille	100 g	4 oz	1/2 cup
Salt	5 ml	1 tsp	1 tsp
Lemon juice	15 ml	1 tbsp	1 tbsp
Canned pineapple	8 chunks	8 chunks	8 chunks
Sugar	5 ml	1 tsp	1 tsp
Chopped coriander (cilantro) leaves	15 ml	1 tbsp	1 tbsp

1. Cut the chicken into 8-12 pieces.

2. Warm the lentils in a saucepan, with a little water if necessary, and simmer for a few minutes until tender and mushy. Then push through a sieve.

3. Heat the oil and add the Basic Curry Sauce. Cook for 2 minutes.

4. Add the chicken and cook for 7 minutes or until tender.

5. Add the ratatouille, 85 ml/3 fl oz/5 1/2 tbsp of water, salt and the cooked lentils. Stir and heat through for 3 minutes.

6. Add the lemon juice, pineapple, sugar and coriander leaves and heat through for about 3 minutes.

 Preparation time: 5 minutes
Cooking time: 20 minutes

Lamb Dhansak

Follow the recipe for Chicken Dhansak but substitute 225 g/ 8 oz of precooked lamb for the chicken at step 4 and cook for 4 minutes instead of 7 minutes.

Keema Dhansak

Follow the recipe for Chicken Dhansak but substitute 225 g/ 8 oz/1 cup of raw minced (ground) beef for the chicken at step 4.

Prawn Dhansak

Follow the recipe for Chicken Dhansak but substitute 225 g/ 8 oz/1 cup of prawns (shrimp) or king prawns for the chicken at step 4 and cook for 3 minutes instead of 7 minutes.

CHICKEN CURRY

This is a medium-hot curry with a smooth sauce.

Serves 2	Metric	Imperial	American
Chicken breast	*225 g*	*8 oz*	*¹/₂ lb*
For the sauce			
Oil	*30 ml*	*2 tbsp*	*2 tbsp*
Curry paste	*15 ml*	*1 tbsp*	*1 tbsp*
Basic Curry Sauce			
(page 22)	*150 ml*	*¹/₄ pt*	*²/₃ cup*
Sugar	*5 ml*	*1 tsp*	*1 tsp*
Salt	*5 ml*	*1 tsp*	*1 tsp*
Finely chopped coriander			
(cilantro) leaves	*15 ml*	*1 tbsp*	*1 tbsp*

1. Cut the chicken into 8 pieces.

2. Heat the oil. Mix the curry paste with 30 ml/2 tbsp water, add to the oil and cook for about 1 minute.

3. Add the Basic Curry Sauce and the chicken and cook until tender for about 7 minutes.

4. Finally, add the sugar, salt and coriander leaves.

5. Instead of Basic Curry Sauce or Basic Curry Paste Sauce you can use 150 ml/¹/₄ pt/²/₃ cup of Onion Purée (page 24), and double the amount of curry paste to 30 ml/2 tbsp.

 Preparation time: 5 minutes
Cooking time: 10 minutes

Lamb Curry

Follow the recipe for Chicken Curry but substitute 225 g/ 8 oz of precooked lamb for the chicken at step 3 and cook for only 3 minutes instead of 7 minutes.

Keema Curry

Follow the recipe for Chicken Curry but add 225 g/8 oz/ 1 cup of raw minced (ground) beef at step 2 and cook for 5 minutes. Omit the chicken at step 3 and reduce the cooking time to 4 minutes.

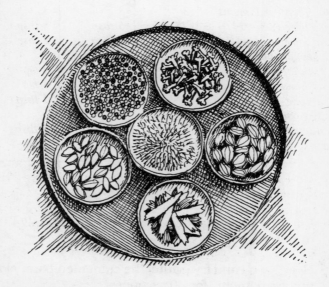

Chicken Bhuna

Bhuna dishes are medium in strength and garnished with onion and tomato.

Serves 2	Metric	Imperial	American
Chicken breast	225 g	8 oz	1/2 lb
For the sauce			
Garlic powder	5 ml	1 tsp	1 tsp
Chilli powder	5 ml	1 tsp	1 tsp
Ground coriander (cilantro)	10 ml	2 tsp	2 tsp
Ground cumin	10 ml	2 tsp	2 tsp
Ground turmeric	5 ml	1 tsp	1 tsp
Oil	30 ml	2 tbsp	2 tbsp
Piece of cinnamon bark	2.5 cm	1 in	1 in
Whole cloves	3	3	3
Whole green cardamoms	3	3	3
Onion Purée (page 24)	75 ml	5 tbsp	5 tbsp
Tomato purée (paste)	30 ml	2 tbsp	2 tbsp
Tomatoes, chopped	2	2	2
Salt	5 ml	1 tsp	1 tsp
Ground black pepper	5 ml	1 tsp	1 tsp
Lemon juice	15 ml	1 tbsp	1 tbsp
Chopped coriander (cilantro) leaves	15 ml	1 tbsp	1 tbsp
Sugar	5 ml	1 tsp	1 tsp

1. Cut the chicken into 8-12 pieces.

2. Put all the ground spices in a cup with 60 ml/4 tbsp of water.

3. Heat the oil and fry (sauté) the cinnamon bark, cloves and cardamoms for 30 seconds.

4. Add the Onion Purée, tomato purée and the spices from the cup and stir for 2 minutes.

5. Add the chicken and cook until tender for about 7 minutes. Add the tomato, 85 ml/3 fl oz/5^1/$_2$ tbsp of water, salt, pepper and lemon juice. Cook for about 5 minutes.

6. Finally, add the coriander leaves and sugar.

Preparation time: 10 minutes
Cooking time: 5 minutes

Lamb Bhuna

Follow the recipe for Chicken Bhuna but substitute 225 g/ 8 oz of precooked lamb for the chicken at step 5 and heat through for only 5 minutes.

Keema Bhuna

Follow the recipe for Chicken Bhuna but add 225 g/8 oz/ 1 cup of raw minced (ground) beef at step 3 and omit the chicken at step 5.

Prawn Bhuna

Follow the recipe for Chicken Bhuna but substitute 225 g/ 8 oz of prawns (shrimp) or king prawns for the chicken at step 5, and cook for about 5 minutes until the prawns are ready.

CHICKEN KORMA

Korma dishes are very mild with a rich, creamy texture, prepared with spices, coconut cream, yoghurt, almonds and sultanas.

Serves 2	Metric	Imperial	American
Chicken breast	225 g	8 oz	1/2 lb
For the sauce			
Korma Curry Powder (page 18)	20 ml	4 tsp	4 tsp
Garlic powder	10 ml	2 tsp	2 tsp
Ground coriander (cilantro)	5 ml	1 tsp	1 tsp
Oil	30 ml	2 tbsp	2 tbsp
Whole cloves	2	2	2
Piece of cinnamon bark	2.5 cm	1 in	1 in
Onion Purée (page 24)	75 ml	5 tbsp	5 tbsp
Natural (plain) yoghurt	15 ml	1 tbsp	1 tbsp
Sugar	5 ml	1 tsp	1 tsp
Salt	5 ml	1 tsp	1 tsp
Sultanas (golden raisins)	15 ml	1 tbsp	1 tbsp
Flaked almonds	15 ml	1 tbsp	1 tbsp
Creamed coconut, grated	25 g	1 oz	1 oz
Cream	30 ml	2 tbsp	2 tbsp
Chopped coriander (cilantro) leaves	15 ml	1 tbsp	1 tbsp

1. Cut the chicken into about 12 cubes.

2. Put the korma curry powder, garlic powder and ground coriander in a cup and mix with 45 ml/3 tbsp of water.

3. Heat the oil and fry (sauté) the cloves and cinnamon bark for 30 seconds.

4. Add the Onion Purée and spices from the cup and stir-fry for about 2 minutes.

5.   Add the chicken and cook until tender for about 7 minutes.

6.   Add the yoghurt and mix well. Add the sugar, salt, sultanas and almonds and stir for about 1 minute.

7.   Finally, mix the creamed coconut with 45 ml/3 tbsp of boiling water and stir into the sauce along with the cream and the coriander leaves. Heat through gently.

Preparation time: 10 minutes
Cooking time: 15 minutes

Lamb Korma

Follow the recipe for Chicken Korma but add 225 g/8 oz of precooked lamb at step 3. Omit step 5.

Keema Korma

Follow the recipe for Chicken Korma but add 225 g/8 oz/ 1 cup of raw minced (ground) beef at step 3 and cook for 7 minutes instead of 30 seconds. Omit step 5.

Prawn or King Prawn Korma

Follow the recipe for Chicken Korma but add 225 g/8 oz/ 1 cup of prawns (shrimp) or king prawns at step 3 and cook for 5 minutes instead of 30 seconds. Omit step 5.

CHICKEN MADRAS

Madras dishes are hot curries of chicken, lamb, beef or prawn with a rich combination of tomato, lemon juice and spices.

Serves 2	Metric	Imperial	American
Chicken breast, precooked	*225 g*	*8 oz*	*¹/₂ lb*
For the sauce			
Oil	*30 ml*	*2 tbsp*	*2 tbsp*
Madras Curry Powder			
(page 17)	*10 ml*	*2 tsp*	*2 tsp*
Chilli powder	*5 ml*	*1 tsp*	*1 tsp*
Sugar	*5 ml*	*1 tsp*	*1 tsp*
Salt	*5 ml*	*1 tsp*	*1 tsp*
Basic Curry Sauce			
(page 22)	*75 ml*	*5 tbsp*	*5 tbsp*
Tomato purée (paste)	*20 ml*	*4 tsp*	*4 tsp*
Lemon juice	*15 ml*	*1 tbsp*	*1 tbsp*
Garam masala	*5 ml*	*1 tsp*	*1 tsp*
Tomatoes, quartered	*2*	*2*	*2*
Chopped coriander			
(cilantro) leaves	*30 ml*	*2 tbsp*	*2 tbsp*

1. Heat the oil, add the curry powder and 15 ml/1 tbsp water, and stir-fry for about 30 seconds along with the chilli powder, sugar and salt.

2. Add the Basic Curry Sauce and tomato purée and cook for 2 minutes.

3. Add the chicken, lemon juice, garam masala and tomatoes and cook for about 3 minutes. Finally, add the coriander leaves.

 Preparation time: 5 minutes
Cooking time: 10 minutes

Lamb Madras

Follow the recipe for Chicken Madras but substitute 225 g/ 8 oz of precooked lamb for the chicken at step 3.

Keema Madras

Follow the recipe for Chicken Madras but substitute 225 g/ 8 oz/1 cup of raw minced (ground) beef for the chicken at step 3 and cook for 7 minutes.

Prawn Madras

Follow the recipe for Chicken Madras, but add 225 g/8 oz / 1 cup of prawns (shrimp) or king prawns at step 1 and cook for 5 minutes. Omit the chicken at step 3.

CHICKEN VINDALOO

Vindaloo dishes are similar to Madras in style, but hotter.

Serves 2	Metric	Imperial	American
Chicken breast, precooked and cubed	225 g	8 oz	¹/₂ lb
For the sauce			
Garlic powder	15 ml	1 tbsp	1 tbsp
Coarsely ground black pepper	5 ml	1 tsp	1 tsp
Ground ginger	5 ml	1 tsp	1 tsp
Chilli powder	5 ml	1 tsp	1 tsp
Vinegar	15 ml	1 tbsp	1 tbsp
Oil	30 ml	2 tbsp	2 tbsp
Thinly sliced onion	100 g	4 oz	1 cup
Tomato purée (paste)	30 ml	2 tbsp	2 tbsp
Lemon juice	15 ml	1 tbsp	1 tbsp
Basic Curry Sauce (page 22)	75 ml	5 tbsp	5 tbsp
Chopped coriander (cilantro) leaves	15 ml	1 tbsp	1 tbsp

1. Put the garlic powder, pepper, ginger and chilli powder in a cup and add the vinegar and 30 ml/2 tbsp of water.

2. Heat the oil and fry (sauté) the onion until golden brown. Add the spices from the cup along with the tomato purée and lemon juice. Stir-fry for 1 minute.

3. Add the chicken and the Basic Curry Sauce and heat through for about 5 minutes.

4. Add the coriander leaves and mix in thoroughly.

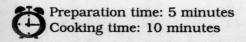 Preparation time: 5 minutes
Cooking time: 10 minutes

Lamb Vindaloo

Follow the recipe for Chicken Vindaloo but substitute 225 g/
8 oz of precooked lamb for the chicken at step 3.

Keema Vindaloo

Follow the recipe for Chicken Vindaloo but add 225 g/8 oz/
1 cup of raw minced (ground) beef at step 2 and stir-fry for
about 5 minutes instead of 1 minute. Omit the chicken at
step 3.

Prawn Vindaloo

Follow the recipe for Chicken Vindaloo but substitute 225 g/
8 oz/1 cup of prawns (shrimp) or king prawns for the
chicken at step 3.

KOFTA

Spiced meatballs cooked in sauce. You can use any cream for this recipe.

Serves 2	Metric	Imperial	American
For the meatballs			
Lean minced (ground) lamb			
OR beef	*350 g*	*12 oz*	*1 ¹/₂ cups*
Salt	*5 ml*	*1 tsp*	*1 tsp*
Garlic powder	*5 ml*	*1 tsp*	*1 tsp*
Large pinch of ground			
ginger			
Kofta powder	*10 ml*	*2 tsp*	*2 tsp*
For the sauce			
Oil	*30 ml*	*2 tbsp*	*2 tbsp*
Basic Curry Sauce			
(page 22)	*75 ml*	*5 tbsp*	*5 tbsp*
Tomato purée (paste)	*10 ml*	*2 tsp*	*2 tsp*
Curry paste	*10 ml*	*2 tsp*	*2 tsp*
Cream	*30 ml*	*2 tbsp*	*2 tbsp*
Chopped coriander			
(cilantro) leaves	*15 ml*	*1 tbsp*	*1 tbsp*

1. Mix the mince, salt and spices together and knead well for about 2 minutes, using your hands, or process in a food processor for 15 seconds.

2. Form into 12 balls. Keep to one side.

3. Heat the oil and cook the Basic Curry Sauce for about 1 minute.

4. Add the tomato purée and curry paste and cook for 1 minute.

5. Add about 45 ml/3 tbsp of water, bring to the boil, add the meat balls and simmer uncovered for about 20 minutes. Add more water during cooking if necessary. Shake the pan from time to time but don't stir or the balls may break up.

6. Finally, stir in the cream and the coriander leaves.

Preparation time: 10 minutes
Cooking time: 30 minutes

NARGISI KOFTA

Boiled egg with spiced minced meat, fried and served in spiced sauce.

Serves 2	Metric	Imperial	American
Sheek Kebab mix (page 36), uncooked	1 recipe	1 recipe	1 recipe
Hard-boiled (hard-cooked) eggs, shelled	2	2	2
Chicken Tikka Masala Sauce (page 80) or any curry sauce	1 recipe	1 recipe	1 recipe
Oil	30 ml	2 tbsp	2 tbsp

1. Divide the Sheek Kebab mixture in two and carefully wrap it around the two eggs.

2. Place the sauce in a pan and heat gently.

3. Heat the oil and carefully fry the eggs for about 10 minutes until brown. When cooked, cut in half, place in the sauce, and heat through for 10-15 minutes.

Preparation time: 10 minutes
Cooking time: 25 minutes

Biryani Dishes & Pilaus

Biryani dishes are complete in themselves: the main ingredient is mixed with the rice and often served with a vegetable curry sauce. Pilau rice dishes make a pleasant change from plain rice, and you can add other ingredients to make them into a complete meal.

CHICKEN BIRYANI

Saffron-coloured rice with chicken, spices and herbs, served with almonds, sultanas and coconut.

Serves 2	Metric	Imperial	American
Chicken breast, precooked	100 g	4 oz	¹/₄ lb
Ghee OR butter	30 ml	2 tbsp	2 tbsp
Thinly sliced onion	100 g	4 oz	1 cup
Whole cloves	2	2	2
Piece of cinnamon bark	2.5 cm	1 in	1 in
Curry paste	5 ml	1 tsp	1 tsp
Plain Boiled Rice (page 130)	225 g	8 oz	¹/₂ lb
Chopped coriander (cilantro) leaves	15 ml	1 tbsp	1 tbsp
Sultanas (golden raisins)	25 g	1 oz	2 tbsp
Salt	5 ml	1 tsp	1 tsp
Flaked almonds	15 ml	1 tbsp	1 tbsp
Desiccated coconut	15 ml	1 tbsp	1 tbsp

1. Tear the chicken breast into bite-sized pieces.

2. Heat the fat and fry (sauté) the onion until golden brown, along with the cloves and cinnamon bark.

3. Mix the curry paste with 15 ml/1 tbsp of water and add to the onion. Stir-fry for 1 minute.

4. Add the chicken and heat through for about 3 minutes.

5. Add the cooked rice, coriander leaves, sultanas, salt and almonds. Stir and heat through thoroughly. Garnish with the desiccated coconut.

6. Serve with the sauce of your choice.

Preparation time: 5 minutes
Cooking time: 15 minutes

Chicken Tikka Biryani

Saffron-coloured rice with chicken tikka, spices and herbs, served with almonds, sultanas and coconut.

Follow the recipe for Chicken Biryani but use precooked Chicken Tikka (page 34) at step 4.

LAMB BIRYANI

Saffron-coloured rice with lamb, spices and herbs, decorated with toasted coconut.

Serves 2	Metric	Imperial	American
Ghee OR butter	30 ml	2 tbsp	2 tbsp
Thinly sliced onion	100 g	4 oz	1 cup
Lamb, precooked	100 g	4 oz	$^1/_4$ lb
Curry paste	5 ml	1 tsp	1 tsp
Ground coriander (cilantro)	5 ml	1 tsp	1 tsp
Ground cumin	5 ml	1 tsp	1 tsp
Tomato, finely chopped	1	1	1
Salt	5 ml	1 tsp	1 tsp
Sultanas (golden raisins)	25 g	1 oz	2 tbsp
Plain Boiled Rice (page 130), cooked	225 g	8 oz	$^1/_2$ lb
Finely chopped coriander (cilantro) leaves	45 ml	3 tbsp	3 tbsp
Toasted desiccated coconut	15 ml	1 tbsp	1 tbsp

1. Heat the fat and fry (sauté) the onion until golden brown.

2. Mix the curry paste with 15 ml/1 tbsp of water and add to the onion along with the lamb, ground coriander, cumin, tomato and salt. Stir-fry for about 5 minutes.

3. Add the sultanas, rice and coriander leaves and heat through.

4. Garnish with the toasted desiccated coconut.

Preparation time: 5 minutes
Cooking time: 15 minutes

Keema Biryani

Saffron-coloured rice with minced meat, spices and herbs, decorated with toasted coconut.

Follow the recipe for Lamb Biryani (page 70) but substitute 100 g/4 oz/^{1}/$_2$ cup of cooked minced (ground) beef for the lamb.

SIMPLE PILAU

Spiced cooked rice.

Serves 2	Metric	Imperial	American
Basmati rice	175 g	6 oz	3/4 cup
Oil	15 ml	1 tbsp	1 tbsp
Finely chopped onion	75 g	3 oz	2/3 cup
Large pinch of garam masala			
Piece of cinnamon bark	2.5 cm	1 in	1 in
Peas	50 g	2 oz	1/2 cup
Salt	5 ml	1 tsp	1 tsp

1. Wash the rice and soak for 30 minutes, then drain.

2. Heat the oil and fry (sauté) the onions until dark reddish-brown.

3. Add about 45 ml/3 tbsp of water and boil for a few minutes to bring out the colour of the onion.

4. Add the garam masala, cinnamon bark, peas, rice and salt. Add 350 ml/12 fl oz/1 1/2 cups of water and bring to the boil, lower the heat to medium and cook until the water has evaporated completely. Cover and leave to rest for about 5 minutes, then stir with a fork.

5. The rice can be kept covered in a cool oven (140°C/275°F/gas mark 1) or warming drawer for up to an hour before serving.

Preparation time: 5 minutes
Cooking time: 20 minutes

MOUGHAL FAMILY PILAU

Brown-coloured rice cooked with cardamom, meat and whole spices.

Serves 2	Metric	Imperial	American
Basmati rice	175 g	6 oz	$^3/_4$ cup
Oil	30 ml	2 tbsp	2 tbsp
Thinly sliced onion	75 g	3 oz	$^2/_3$ cup
Whole peppercorns	6	6	6
Piece of cinnamon bark	2.5 cm	1 in	1 in
Whole cloves	3	3	3
Whole brown cardamom	1	1	1
Lamb OR chicken, precooked	225 g	8 oz	$^1/_2$ lb

1. Wash the rice and soak for 30 minutes, then drain.

2. Heat the oil and fry (sauté) the onion along with the peppercorns, cinnamon bark, cloves and cardamom until the onion is dark reddish-brown. Add the meat and fry until the meat browns a little, stirring all the time.

3. Add 120 ml/4 fl oz/$^1/_2$ cup of water and cook for 2 minutes to bring out the colour of the onion. Bring to the boil and stir until the liquid reduces by half.

4. Add the rice, salt and 350 ml/12 fl oz/$1^1/_2$ cups of water. Bring to the boil, lower the heat to medium and cook until the water has evaporated. Cover and leave to rest for 5 minutes, then stir with a fork.

5. The rice can be kept covered in a cool oven (140°C/275°F/gas mark 1) for up to an hour before serving.

Preparation time: 5 minutes
Cooking time: 20 minutes

PRAWN PILAU

Rice cooked with prawns, herbs and spices.

Serves 2	Metric	Imperial	American
Oil	30 ml	2 tbsp	2 tbsp
Flaked almonds	25 g	1 oz	1 oz
Finely chopped onion	100 g	4 oz	1 cup
Tomato, chopped	1 large	1 large	1 large
Sultanas (golden raisins)	50 g	2 oz	$^1/_3$ cup
Prawns (shrimp)	225 g	8 oz	$^1/_2$ lb
Large pinch of ground turmeric			
Plain Boiled Rice (page 130)	225 g	8 oz	2 cups
Sugar	5 ml	1 tsp	1 tsp
Salt	5 ml	1 tsp	1 tsp

1. Heat the oil and fry (sauté) the almonds until golden, then remove and keep to one side.

2. Add the onion to the oil and fry until golden brown. Add the tomato and sultanas and fry for about 3 minutes.

3. Add the prawns and cook for 3 minutes.

4. Add the turmeric, cooked rice, sugar and salt and mix thoroughly. Heat through.

5. The rice can be kept covered in a cool oven (140°C/275°F/gas mark 1) or warming drawer for up to an hour before serving.

Preparation time: 5 minutes
Cooking time: 20 minutes

SHAHJAHANI PILAU

Serves 2	Metric	Imperial	American
Prawn Pilau (page 74)	1 recipe	1 recipe	1 recipe
Lamb Tikka (page 33), precooked	50 g	2 oz	2 oz
Tandoori Chicken (page 30), precooked	50 g	2 oz	2 oz

1.   Follow the recipe for Prawn Pilau and add the lamb and chicken with the prawns at step 3.

2.   Serve with a curry sauce.

Preparation time: 5 minutes
Cooking time: 20 minutes

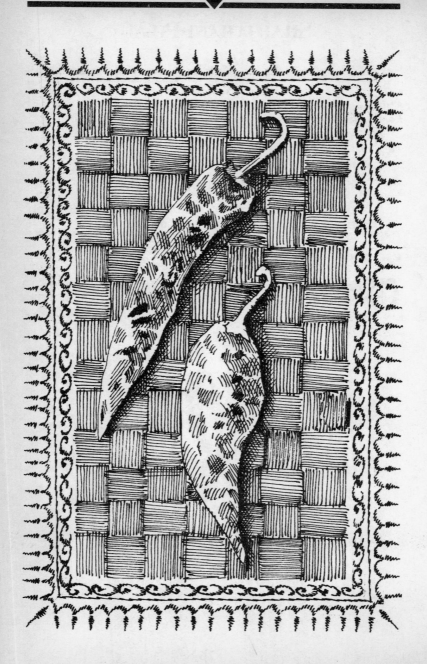

Chef's Recommendations

Here are some of my favourite dishes based on those you can find on restaurant and take-away menus. You can combine a few dishes if you want to make a special meal, or simply select one of your favourites and serve it with rice or bread.

BUTTERED CHICKEN BREAST

Tandoori chicken breast cooked in butter and spiced sauce. Use any cream for this recipe.

Serves 2	Metric	Imperial	American
Butter	*25 g*	*1 oz*	*2 tbsp*
Whole green cardamoms	*2*	*2*	*2*
Piece of cinnamon bark	*2.5 cm*	*1 in*	*1 in*
Whole cloves	*2*	*2*	*2*
Tandoori Chicken (page 30), precooked	*2 breasts*	*2 breasts*	*2 breasts*
Cream	*30 ml*	*2 tbsp*	*2 tbsp*
Salt	*5 ml*	*1 tsp*	*1 tsp*

1. Melt the butter in a pan and fry (sauté) the cardamoms, cinnamon bark and cloves for about 30 seconds.

2. Add the chicken breasts and heat through.

3. Add the cream and salt and cook for 1-2 minutes over a gentle heat. Do not boil.

4. Serve with Naan Bread (page 132) and Simple Pilau (page 72).

Preparation time: 5 minutes
Cooking time: 10 minutes

SPECIAL TANDOORI MIX

Pieces of tandoori chicken, chicken tikka, sheek kebab and shami kebab served with naan bread and curry sauce.

Serves 2	Metric	Imperial	American
Tandoori Chicken (page 30), precooked	*2 pieces*	*2 pieces*	*2 pieces*
Chicken Tikka (page 34), precooked	*2 pieces*	*2 pieces*	*2 pieces*
Sheek Kebab (page 36), precooked	*2 pieces*	*2 pieces*	*2 pieces*
Mild Shami Kebab (page 38), precooked	*2 pieces*	*2 pieces*	*2 pieces*
Basic Curry Sauce (page 22)	*75 ml*	*5 tbsp*	*5 tbsp*
Naan Bread (page 132)	*2*	*2*	*2*
Simple Pilau (page 72) (optional)	*1 recipe*	*1 recipe*	*1 recipe*

1. Heat the Tandoori Chicken, Chicken Tikka, Sheek Kebab and Shami Kebab on a baking tray in the oven for about 15 minutes at 180°C/350°F/gas mark 4.

2. Heat through the Basic Curry Sauce in a saucepan.

3. Wrap the Naan Bread in foil and heat in the oven for 10 minutes only.

4. The Simple Pilau, if used, can be covered and reheated in the same oven.

5. Serve the Basic Curry Sauce either separately or poured over the meats.

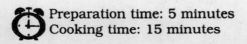

Preparation time: 5 minutes
Cooking time: 15 minutes

CHICKEN TIKKA MASALA

Marinated chicken in a spiced cream sauce. Any type of cream is fine.

Serves 2	Metric	Imperial	American
Oil	30 ml	2 tbsp	2 tbsp
Basic Curry Sauce (page 22)	75 ml	5 tbsp	5 tbsp
Sugar	10 ml	2 tsp	2 tsp
Finely chopped coriander (cilantro) leaves	15 ml	1 tbsp	1 tbsp
Tandoori powder or paste	5 ml	1 tsp	1 tsp
Tomato purée (paste)	5 ml	1 tsp	1 tsp
Mint sauce	5 ml	1 tsp	1 tsp
Salt	5 ml	1 tsp	1 tsp
Chicken Tikka (page 34), precooked	225 g	8 oz	8 oz
Cream	45 ml	3 tbsp	3 tbsp

1. Heat the oil in a pan and cook the Basic Curry Sauce over medium heat for about 2 minutes.

2. Add the sugar, coriander leaves, tandoori powder or paste, tomato purée, mint sauce and salt. Stir well.

3. Add the Chicken Tikka and cook for about 5 minutes until heated through.

4. Add the cream and mix in thoroughly.

5. Serve with Plain Boiled Rice (page 130).

Preparation time: 5 minutes
Cooking time: 15 minutes

Lamb Tikka Masala

Marinated lamb in a spiced sauce.

Follow the recipe for Chicken Tikka Masala but substitute 225 g/8 oz of precooked Lamb Tikka (page 33) for the chicken at step 3.

Fish Tikka Masala

Marinated cod in a spiced cream sauce.

Follow the recipe for Chicken Tikka Masala but substitute 225 g/8 oz of precooked Fish Tikka (page 35) for the chicken at step 3, and stir in another 30 ml/2 tbsp finely chopped coriander (cilantro) leaves just before serving.

King Prawn Tikka Masala

Marinated prawns in a spiced cream sauce.

Follow the recipe for Chicken Tikka Masala but substitute 225 g/8 oz/1 cup of precooked King Prawn Tikka (see page 35) for the chicken at step 3, and stir in another 30 ml/2 tbsp finely chopped coriander (cilantro) leaves just before serving. Serve with Plain Boiled Rice (page 130) and lemon wedges.

TANDOORI CHICKEN MASALA

Marinated chicken cooked with cream and spices. Use whatever cream you prefer.

Serves 2	Metric	Imperial	American
Tandoori Chicken (page 30), precooked	225 g	8 oz	1/2 lb
For the sauce			
Tandoori powder or paste	5 ml	1 tsp	1 tsp
Natural (plain) yoghurt	30 ml	2 tbsp	2 tbsp
Oil	30 ml	2 tbsp	2 tbsp
Basic Curry Sauce (page 22)	75 ml	5 tbsp	5 tbsp
Tomato, finely chopped	1	1	1
Sugar	10 ml	2 tsp	2 tsp
Dried fenugreek	5 ml	1 tsp	1 tsp
Ground almonds	15 ml	1 tbsp	1 tbsp
Cream	30 ml	2 tbsp	2 tbsp

1. Mix together the tandoori powder or paste and yoghurt.

2. Heat the oil in a pan and add the Basic Curry Sauce. Cook over medium heat for about 2 minutes.

3. Add the yoghurt mixture and cook for a further 30 seconds.

4. Add the tomato and chicken and simmer for about 5 minutes until the chicken is heated through.

5. Add the sugar, fenugreek, almonds and cream and stir well. Heat through without boiling. Add a little water if the sauce seems too thick.

6. Serve with Simple Pilau (page 72) or Naan Bread (page 132).

Preparation time: 5 minutes
Cooking time: 15 minutes

King Prawn Tandoori Masala

Marinated prawns cooked with cream and spices.

Follow the recipe for Tandoori Chicken Masala but substitute 225 g/8 oz/1 cup of Tandoori King Prawns (page 32) for the chicken at step 4.

Sheek Kebab Masala

Kebabs marinated in yoghurt and spices.

Follow the recipe for Tandoori Chicken Masala but substitute four precooked Sheek Kebabs (page 36) for the chicken at step 4.

As an alternative, serve two Sheek Kebabs and add one hard-boiled egg, halved lengthways, to the sauce at the same time as the cream.

LAMB CHOPS MASALA

Lamb chops marinated in yoghurt and spices.

Serves 2	Metric	Imperial	American
Natural (plain) yoghurt	150 ml	1/4 pt	2/3 cup
Oil	15 ml	1 tbsp	1 tbsp
Ground ginger	5 ml	1 tsp	1 tsp
Garlic powder	5 ml	1 tsp	1 tsp
Chilli powder	5 ml	1 tsp	1 tsp
Ground cumin	5 ml	1 tsp	1 tsp
Salt	5 ml	1 tsp	1 tsp
Coarsely ground black pepper	5 ml	1 tsp	1 tsp
Lamb chops, washed and dried	225 g	8 oz	1/2 lb

1. Mix together all the ingredients except the chops.

2. Coat the chops in the yoghurt mixture, using your hands.

3. Cover and leave to marinate in the fridge for several hours or preferably overnight.

4. Place the chops on a baking sheet and cook under a preheated grill (broiler) for about 7 minutes each side, or cook in an oven preheated to 190°C/375°F/gas mark 5 for about 30 minutes, turning half way through.

5. Serve with Simple Indian Salad (page 141) and chutney.

Preparation time: 5 minutes
Cooking time: 10 minutes

CHICKEN TIKKA KEEMA MASALA

Chicken in spiced minced meat sauce. You can use any type of cream.

Serves 2	Metric	Imperial	American
Oil	15 ml	1 tbsp	1 tbsp
Kebab (page 36) or Kofta (page 64) mix, uncooked	50 g	2 oz	1/2 cup
Basic Curry Sauce (page 22)	75 ml	5 tbsp	5 tbsp
Chicken Tikka (page 34), precooked	225 g	8 oz	1/2 lb
Salt	5 ml	1 tsp	1 tsp
Sugar	5 ml	1 tsp	1 tsp
Chopped coriander (cilantro) leaves	15 ml	1 tbsp	1 tbsp
Cream	30 ml	2 tbsp	2 tbsp

1. Heat the oil and fry (sauté) the Kebab or Kofta mix until cooked and well broken up.

2. Add the Basic Curry Sauce and cook for about 3 minutes.

3. Add the Chicken Tikka, salt, sugar and coriander leaves and cook for about 5 minutes to heat through.

4. Finally, add the cream and heat through gently.

Preparation time: 5 minutes
Cooking time: 10 minutes

CHICKEN PASANDA

Chicken in a rich almond and cream sauce. Use whatever type of cream you prepfer.

Serves 2	Metric	Imperial	American
Garlic powder	5 ml	1 tsp	1 tsp
Large pinch of ground cardamom			
Ground coriander (cilantro)	5 ml	1 tsp	1 tsp
Large pinch of garam masala			
Large pinch of chilli powder			
Ground cumin	5 ml	1 tsp	1 tsp
Paprika	5 ml	1 tsp	1 tsp
Large pinch of ground turmeric			
Chicken breast	225 g	8 oz	1/2 lb
Oil	30 ml	2 tbsp	2 tbsp
Onion Purée (page 24)	75 ml	5 tbsp	5 tbsp
Finely chopped coriander (cilantro) leaves	30 ml	2 tbsp	2 tbsp
Sugar	10 ml	2 tsp	2 tsp
Salt	5 ml	1 tsp	1 tsp
Ground almonds	30 ml	2 tbsp	2 tbsp
Cream	60 ml	4 tbsp	4 tbsp

1. Put the garlic powder, cardamom, ground coriander, garam masala, chilli powder, cumin, paprika and turmeric in a cup and add 45 ml/3 tbsp water.

2. Cut the chicken breast into about eight pieces. Flatten slightly.

3. Heat the oil and add the Onion Purée and spice mix from the cup. Cook over medium heat for about 2 minutes.

4. Add the chicken pieces and cook for about 7 minutes until cooked, stirring constantly. If the sauce looks too thick, thin by adding water.

5. Add the coriander leaves, sugar, salt and ground almonds and stir well. Finally, add the cream and heat through gently.

 Preparation time: 10 minutes
Cooking time: 15 minutes

Lamb Pasanda

Lamb in a rich almond and cream sauce.

Follow the recipe for Chicken Pasanda but substitute 225 g/ 8 oz of slightly flattened precooked lamb for the chicken at stage 4 and heat through for about 5 minutes.

CHINGRI PURI

Fried puri with prawn stuffing.

Serves 2	Metric	Imperial	American
For the puri			
Puri (page 135)	$^1/_2$ recipe	$^1/_2$ recipe	$^1/_2$ recipe
Oil for frying			
For the filling			
Oil	30 ml	2 tbsp	2 tbsp
Thinly sliced onion	50 g	2 oz	$^1/_2$ cup
Garlic clove, finely chopped	1	1	1
Curry paste	10 ml	2 tsp	2 tsp
Pinch of ground ginger			
Basic Curry Sauce (page 22)	30 ml	2 tbsp	2 tbsp
Frozen prawns (shrimp), thawed	100 g	4 oz	$^1/_4$ lb
Chopped coriander (cilantro) leaves	15 ml	1 tbsp	1 tbsp
Salt	5 ml	1 tsp	1 tsp
Sugar	5 ml	1 tsp	1 tsp

1. Heat the oil for the filling in a pan, add the onion and fry (sauté) until golden brown. Add the garlic and cook for 1 minute, then add the curry paste, ginger and Basic Curry Sauce and mix well together.

2. Add the prawns and cook for about 3 minutes. Stir in the coriander leaves, salt and sugar. Set aside until completely cold.

3. Divide the puri dough into two portions and roll each out into a 23 cm/9 in circle.

4. Place half of the filling on each circle. Brush the edges with water, fold each in half to form two half-circles and seal well. Flatten slightly.

5. Heat half the oil in a large frying pan (skillet) and fry (sauté) one puri over a moderate heat for approximately 2 minutes. Repeat for the second puri.

Preparation time: 5 minutes
Cooking time: 10 minutes

KARHAI CHICKEN

Delicately spiced chicken cooked with cardamom, tomato and yoghurt.

Serves 2	Metric	Imperial	American
Chicken breast	225 g	8 oz	1/2 lb
For the sauce			
Large pinch of ground ginger			
Garlic powder	5 ml	1 tsp	1 tsp
Chilli powder	5 ml	1 tsp	1 tsp
Ground cumin	5 ml	1 tsp	1 tsp
Oil	30 ml	2 tbsp	2 tbsp
Piece of cinnamon bark	2.5 cm	1 in	1 in
Cloves	2	2	2
Whole green cardamoms	2	2	2
Onion Purée (page 24)	75 ml	5 tbsp	5 tbsp
Tomatoes, chopped	2	2	2
Finely chopped coriander (cilantro) leaves	30 ml	2 tbsp	2 tbsp
Natural (plain) yoghurt	30 ml	2 tbsp	2 tbsp
Sugar	10 ml	2 tsp	2 tsp
Salt	5 ml	1 tsp	1 tsp

1. Cut the chicken breast into about 12 pieces.

2. Put the ginger, garlic powder, chilli powder and cumin in a cup and add 30 ml/2 tbsp water.

3. Heat the oil and fry (sauté) the cinnamon bark, cloves and cardamoms for 30 seconds.

4. Add the Onion Purée and the spice mix from the cup and stir-fry over moderate heat for about 2 minutes.

5. Add the chicken pieces and stir-fry for about 7 minutes until tender.

6. Add the tomato and coriander leaves and cook for about 2 minutes.

7. Finally, stir in the yoghurt, sugar and salt and heat through.

Preparation time: 10 minutes
Cooking time: 15 minutes

KARHAI LAMB

Lamb with a smooth, spicy sauce.

Serves 2	Metric	Imperial	American
Lamb, precooked	225 g	8 oz	1/2 lb
For the sauce			
Garlic powder	5 ml	1 tsp	1 tsp
Pinch of ground coriander (cilantro)			
Chilli powder	5 ml	1 tsp	1 tsp
Large pinch of aniseed powder			
Pinch of ground cumin			
Pinch of dried fenugreek leaves			
Oil	30 ml	2 tbsp	2 tbsp
Piece of cinnamon bark	2.5 cm	1 in	1 in
Whole green cardamoms	3 small	3 small	3 small
Basic Curry Paste Sauce (page 23)	75 ml	5 tbsp	5 tbsp
Tomatoes, chopped	2	2	2
Finely chopped coriander (cilantro) leaves	45 ml	3 tbsp	3 tbsp
Sugar	10 ml	2 tsp	2 tsp
Natural (plain) yoghurt	30 ml	2 tbsp	2 tbsp
Salt	5 ml	1 tsp	1 tsp

1. Put the garlic powder, ground coriander , chilli powder, aniseed, cumin and fenugreek in a cup and add 30 ml/ 2 tbsp of water.

2. Heat the oil and fry (sauté) the cinnamon bark and cardamoms for 30 seconds.

3. Add the Basic Curry Paste Sauce and spice mix from the cup and stir-fry for about 2 minutes.

4. Add the precooked meat and heat through for about 5 minutes.

5. Add the tomato and coriander leaves and cook for about 2 minutes.

6. Finally, stir in the sugar, yoghurt and salt and heat through.

Preparation time: 10 minutes
Cooking time: 15 minutes

Karhai Vegetables

Vegetables with a smooth, spicy sauce.

Follow the recipe for Karhai Lamb but substitute 225 g/8 oz of precooked mixed vegetables, such as cauliflower, potato, peas, green beans etc., for the lamb and heat through for about 3 minutes.

PALAK GOSHT

Lamb cooked with spinach.

Serves 2	Metric	Imperial	American
Lamb, precooked	225 g	8 oz	1/2 lb
For the sauce			
Pinch of ground turmeric			
Pinch of ground cinnamon			
Pinch of ground ginger			
Garlic powder	5 ml	1 tsp	1 tsp
Pinch of chilli powder			
Oil	30 ml	2 tbsp	2 tbsp
Onion, halved and thinly sliced	1	1	1
Finely chopped coriander (cilantro) leaves	60 ml	4 tbsp	4 tbsp
Onion Purée (page 24)	75 ml	5 tbsp	5 tbsp
Tomato, finely chopped	1 large	1 large	1 large
Salt	5 ml	1 tsp	1 tsp
Sugar	5 ml	1 tsp	1 tsp
Frozen chopped spinach	100 g	4 oz	4 oz

1. Put the turmeric, cinnamon, ginger, garlic powder and chilli powder in a cup and add 30 ml/2 tbsp of water.

2. Heat the oil and fry (sauté) the sliced onion until golden brown.

3. Add the coriander leaves and fry gently for 2 minutes.

4. Add the spices from the cup and stir-fry for 1 minute.

5. Add the Onion Purée and tomato and stir-fry for 2 minutes.

6. Add the salt, sugar, spinach and meat. Stir well to mix and cook for about 7 minutes until the meat is heated through.

Preparation time: 10 minutes
Cooking time: 15 minutes

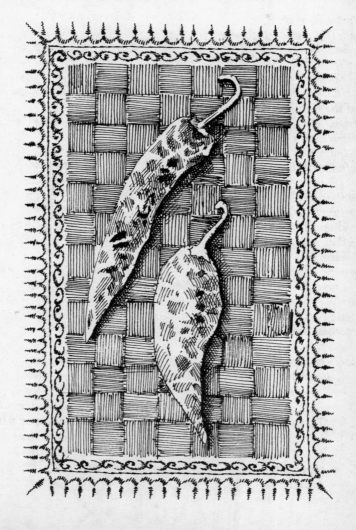

MASALA DOSA

Vegetable-stuffed pancakes.

Serves 2	Metric	Imperial	American
For the pancakes			
Plain (all-purpose) flour			
OR *dosa mix*	100 g	4 oz	1 cup
Pinch of salt			
Egg, beaten	1	1	1
Milk	300 ml	¹/₂ pt	1 ¹/₄ cups
For the filling			
Ground ginger	5 ml	1 tsp	1 tsp
Korma Curry Powder			
(page 18)	5 ml	1 tsp	1 tsp
Garam masala	5 ml	1 tsp	1 tsp
Oil	15 ml	1 tbsp	1 tbsp
Thinly sliced onion	50 g	2 oz	¹/₂ cup
Garlic cloves, finely			
chopped	3	3	3
Mushrooms, sliced	4	4	4
Tomato, chopped	1	1	1
Basic Curry Sauce			
(page 22)	30 ml	2 tbsp	2 tbsp
Salt	5 ml	1 tsp	1 tsp
Sugar	5 ml	1 tsp	1 tsp
Potatoes, cooked and			
roughly chopped	2	2	2
Finely chopped coriander			
(cilantro) leaves	as liked	as liked	as liked

1. To make the pancakes, mix together the flour and
    salt. Add the egg and half the milk. Mix well. Add the
    remaining milk and mix well. The batter should have
    the consistency of double (heavy) cream.

2. Heat a frying pan (skillet). Put about 5 ml/1 tsp of the oil in the pan and rub it over the base with a paper towel. The heat should remain at medium throughout.

3. Place approximately 60 ml/4 tbsp of the batter in the pan and quickly spread it over the base by tilting the pan to give a thin layer. Cook for about 3-4 minutes, then carefully turn and cook the other side for a further 2 minutes.

4. Remove the cooked pancake from the pan and repeat step 3 to make the other pancakes.

5. To make the filling, put the ginger, Korma Curry Powder and garam masala in a cup with 30 ml/2 tbsp of water.

6. Heat the oil. Add the onion and fry (sauté) until golden brown. Add the garlic and fry (sauté) for 1 minute. Add the mushroom and tomato and cook for 2 minutes. Add the spice mix from the cup, the Basic Curry Sauce, salt and sugar and cook for a further 2 minutes. Finally, add the potato and coriander leaves and mix well together.

7. Place about 15 ml/1 tbsp of the mix on each pancake and roll up.

8. Heat through in the oven at 180°C/350°F/gas mark 4 for about 20 minutes before serving.

9. Serve with Yoghurt and Mint Sauce (page 139).

 Preparation time: 10 minutes
Cooking time: 40 minutes

CHICKEN JALFREZI

A hot chicken dish with green chillies, peppers and coriander .

Serves 2	Metric	Imperial	American
Chicken breast	225 g	8 oz	$^1/_2$ lb
For the sauce			
Garlic powder	5 ml	1 tsp	1 tsp
Ground ginger	5 ml	1 tsp	1 tsp
Chilli powder	5 ml	1 tsp	1 tsp
Oil	30 ml	2 tbsp	2 tbsp
Thinly sliced onion	100 g	4 oz	1 cup
Curry paste	10 ml	2 tsp	2 tsp
Onion Purée (page 24)	75 ml	5 tbsp	5 tbsp
Green (bell) pepper, diced	1	1	1
Green chillies, seeded and chopped	4	4	4
Chopped coriander (cilantro) leaves	45 ml	3 tbsp	3 tbsp
Salt	5 ml	1 tsp	1 tsp
Sugar	5 ml	1 tsp	1 tsp

1.   Cut the chicken breast into about eight pieces.

2.   Put the garlic powder, ginger and chilli powder in a cup and add 30 ml/2 tbsp of water.

3.   Heat the oil and fry (sauté) the sliced onion until golden brown.

4.   Add the curry paste and spices from the cup and stir-fry for 1 minute. Add the Onion Purée and cook for a further 1 minute.

5.   Add the chicken and green pepper and cook until the chicken is tender, about 7 minutes.

6. Finally, add the chillies, coriander leaves, salt and sugar and cook for about 2 minutes.

Preparation time: 5 minutes
Cooking time: 20 minutes

MURGH JALFREZI

Chicken stuffed with lemon, butter and garlic.

Serves 2	Metric	Imperial	American
Butter	*25 g*	*1 oz*	*2 tbsp*
Grated lemon zest	*1/2*	*1/2*	*1/2*
Garlic powder	*5 ml*	*1 tsp*	*1 tsp*
Chicken breasts (275 g/			
10 oz total weight)	*2*	*2*	*2*

1. Mix together the butter, lemon zest and garlic powder. Divide into two portions and cool in the fridge for about 30 minutes.

2. Make a pocket along one side of each chicken breast with a sharp knife and stuff with a portion of the garlic butter.

3. Wrap the chicken in foil and bake in the oven at 190°C/375°F/gas mark 5 for approximately 30 minutes. Unwrap the foil for the last 10 minutes to allow the breasts to brown.

Preparation time: 5 minutes plus chilling
Cooking time: 30 minutes

CHINGRI JALFREZI

Prawns with garlic, spices and herbs.

Serves 2	Metric	Imperial	American
Pinch of ground coriander (cilantro)			
Pinch of chilli powder			
Pinch of ground cumin			
Garlic powder	5 ml	1 tsp	1 tsp
Oil	30 ml	2 tbsp	2 tbsp
Onion, finely chopped	100 g	4 oz	1 cup
Fresh ginger, finely chopped	25 g	1 oz	1 oz
Prawns (shrimp)	225 g	8 oz	1/2 lb
Finely chopped tomato	50 g	2 oz	1/4 cup
Spring onions (scallions), finely chopped	75 g	3 oz	2/3 cup
Finely chopped coriander (cilantro) leaves	45 ml	3 tbsp	3 tbsp
Pinch of salt			
Sugar	5 ml	1 tsp	1 tsp

1. Put all the ground spices and garlic powder in a cup and add 15 ml/1 tbsp of water.

2. Heat the oil and fry (sauté) the onion until golden.

3. Add the ginger and cook for 1 minute, then add the spices from the cup and cook for another minute.

4. Add the prawns and tomato and stir-fry for 4 minutes. Add the spring onions, coriander leaves, salt and sugar and cook for about 2 minutes.

 Preparation time: 5 minutes
Cooking time: 15 minutes

KOFTA JALFREZI

Deep-fried spiced meatballs.

Serves 2	Metric	Imperial	American
Pinch of ground cumin			
Ground coriander (cilantro)	*5 ml*	*1 tsp*	*1 tsp*
Pinch of chilli powder			
Garlic powder	*5 ml*	*1 tsp*	*1 tsp*
Kofta powder	*5 ml*	*1 tsp*	*1 tsp*
Minced (ground) beef	*350 g*	*12 oz*	*1 1/2 cups*
Finely chopped coriander			
(cilantro) leaves	*15 ml*	*1 tbsp*	*1 tbsp*
Salt	*5 ml*	*1 tsp*	*1 tsp*
Oil for deep frying			

1. Put all the ground spices and garlic powder in a cup and add 15 ml/1 tbsp of water.

2. Put the mince in a bowl and add the spices from the cup and all the other ingredients. Knead well with your hands or process in a food processor for about 15 seconds.

3. Form into 12 balls and deep fry until golden brown.

4. Serve on their own or with Mild Curry Sauce (page 23).

Preparation time: 10 minutes
Cooking time: 10 minutes

MACHCHI KOFTA

Fish balls with yoghurt and mustard sauce.

Serves 2	Metric	Imperial	American
Yoghurt and Mustard Sauce (page 139)	1 recipe	1 recipe	1 recipe
For the fish balls			
Pinch of ground turmeric			
Pinch of garlic powder			
Pinch of ground coriander (cilantro)			
Pinch of ground cumin			
Pinch of chilli powder			
Oil	30 ml	2 tbsp	2 tbsp
Finely chopped onion	50 g	2 oz	1/2 cup
White fish fillet, cooked	225 g	8 oz	1/2 lb
Cooked mashed potato	225 g	8 oz	8 oz
Finely chopped coriander (cilantro) leaves	15 ml	1 tbsp	1 tbsp
Salt	5 ml	1 tsp	1 tsp
Egg, beaten	1	1	1
Dried breadcrumbs	50 g	2 oz	1/2 cup

1. Place all the ground spices in a cup with 10 ml/2 tsp water.

2. Heat the oil and fry (sauté) the onion until golden brown. Add the spice mix from the cup and cook gently for about 1 minute.

3. Mash the cooked fish and add to the pan. Fry for about 2 minutes.

4. Finally, add the mashed potato, coriander leaves and salt. Allow to cool.

5. Shape into about 16 balls. Dip in the egg and then in the breadcrumbs. Deep fry in batches for about 2 minutes until golden or bake in the oven at 190°C/375°F/gas mark 5 for about 25 minutes.

6. Serve with the Yoghurt and Mustard Sauce.

Preparation time: 10 minutes
Cooking time: 25 minutes

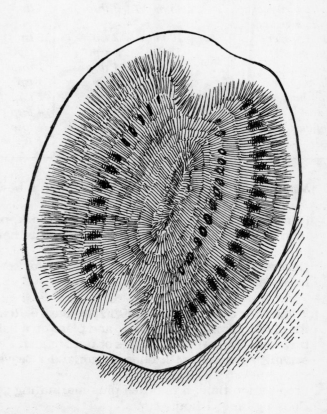

HONEY CHICKEN

Chicken marinated in honey and paprika.

Serves 2	Metric	Imperial	American
Chicken breasts (225 g/8 oz			
total weight)	2	2	2
Oil	*30 ml*	*2 tbsp*	*2 tbsp*
Finely chopped coriander			
(cilantro) leaves	*45 ml*	*3 tbsp*	*3 tbsp*
For the marinade			
Ground ginger	*10 ml*	*2 tsp*	*2 tsp*
Garlic powder	*5 ml*	*1 tsp*	*1 tsp*
Paprika	*15 ml*	*1 tbsp*	*1 tbsp*
Chilli powder	*5 ml*	*1 tsp*	*1 tsp*
Lemon juice	*30 ml*	*2 tbsp*	*2 tbsp*
Honey	*60 ml*	*4 tbsp*	*4 tbsp*
Cornflour (cornstarch)	*15 ml*	*1 tbsp*	*1 tbsp*
Salt	*5 ml*	*1 tsp*	*1 tsp*

1. Mix together the marinade ingredients in a bowl.

2. Prick the chicken breasts all over with a fork, place them in the marinade and coat well using your hands.

3. Cover and leave to marinate in the fridge for several hours or preferably overnight.

4. Preheat the oven to 200°C/400°F/gas mark 6. Remove the chicken from the marinade and place on a baking tray. Cook for 40 to 50 minutes or until tender. Before serving, sprinkle on the chopped coriander leaves.

 Preparation time: 5 minutes plus marinating
Cooking time: 1 hour

PEPPERCORN LAMB

Lean lamb steaks flambéed with whisky. Any type of cream is fine.

Serves 2	Metric	Imperial	American
Lean lamb	225 g	8 oz	1/2 lb
Whole black peppercorns	15 ml	1 tbsp	1 tbsp
Butter	25 g	1 oz	1 oz
Oil	15 ml	1 tbsp	1 tbsp
Whisky	30 ml	2 tbsp	2 tbsp
French mustard	5 ml	1 tsp	1 tsp
Salt	5 ml	1 tsp	1 tsp
Cream	45 ml	3 tbsp	3 tbsp

1. Cut the lamb into 5 cm/2 in cubes and flatten to about 5 mm/^{1}/$_4$ in in thickness.

2. Crush the peppercorns roughly and press well into the lamb on both sides.

3. Heat the butter and oil and fry the lamb pieces for about 6 minutes until cooked.

4. Add the whisky to the pan and set alight. When the flames have died down add the mustard, salt and cream and heat through. Do not boil.

 Preparation time: 5 minutes
Cooking time: 10 minutes

Peppercorn Chicken

Follow the recipe for Peppercorn Lamb above, but use chicken breasts cut into four portions, flattened as for the lamb. Cook for only 5 minutes at step 3.

Moglai Lamb

Lamb cooked with single (light) or double (heavy) cream and egg.

Serves 2	Metric	Imperial	American
Lamb, precooked	225 g	8 oz	1/2 lb
For the sauce			
Oil	30 ml	2 tbsp	2 tbsp
Piece of cinnamon bark	2.5 cm	1 in	1 in
Whole green cardamoms	2	2	2
Basic Curry Sauce			
(page 22)	75 ml	5 tbsp	5 tbsp
Tandoori Powder (page 19)	10 ml	1 tsp	1 tsp
Chopped coriander			
(cilantro) leaves	15 ml	1 tbsp	1 tbsp
Chopped almonds	15 ml	1 tbsp	1 tbsp
Finely chopped green (bell)			
pepper	50 g	2 oz	2 oz
Salt	5 ml	1 tsp	1 tsp
Sugar	5 ml	1 tsp	1 tsp
Cream	50 ml	2 fl oz	3 1/2 tbsp
Hard-boiled (hard-cooked)			
egg, halved lengthways	1	1	1

1. Heat the oil and stir-fry the cinnamon bark and cardamoms for 30 seconds

2. Add the Basic Curry Sauce and Tandoori Powder and cook for 2 minutes.

3. Add the meat and heat through for about 5 minutes.

4. Add the coriander leaves, almonds, green pepper, salt and sugar and mix well.

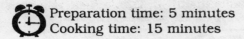

5.   Finally, stir in the cream and egg halves and heat through for about 3-4 minutes without boiling.

Preparation time: 5 minutes
Cooking time: 15 minutes

Moglai Chicken

Tandoori chicken cooked with cream, nuts and egg.

Follow the recipe for Moglai Lamb but substitute 225 g/ 8 oz of precooked Tandoori Chicken Masala (page 82) for the lamb at step 3.

VEGETABLE Dishes

This chapter includes a range of vegetables dishes, and some with egg as well! Of course, you will also find other vegetable variations in the other chapters.

ALOO MATAR

Potato and peas in sauce.

Serves 2	Metric	Imperial	American
Oil	30 ml	2 tbsp	2 tbsp
Basic Curry Sauce (page 22)	75 ml	5 tbsp	5 tbsp
Garlic powder	5 ml	1 tsp	1 tsp
Potato, cooked and quartered	225 g	8 oz	1/2 lb
Frozen peas	50 g	2 oz	1/2 cup
Finely chopped green (bell) pepper	25 g	1 oz	1 oz
Salt	5 ml	1 tsp	2 tsp
Sugar	5 ml	1 tsp	1 tsp

1. Heat the oil and add the Basic Curry Sauce and garlic powder. Cook for about 2 minutes.

2. Add the potato, peas, green pepper, salt and sugar and heat through gently for about 3 minutes.

 Preparation time: 5 minutes
Cooking time: 5 minutes

Vegetable Matar

Follow the recipe for Aloo Matar above and substitute 225 g/ 8 oz/¹/₂ lb of mixed vegetables, such as peas, potato, cauliflower, green beans, for the vegetables at step 2.

ALOO GOBI

Potato and cauliflower in sauce.

Serves 2	Metric	Imperial	American
Oil	30 ml	2 tbsp	2 tbsp
Basic Curry Sauce			
(page 22)	75 ml	5 tbsp	5 tbsp
Potato, cooked and halved	100 g	4 oz	$^{1}/_4$ lb
Cauliflower, cooked	100 g	4 oz	$^{1}/_4$ lb
Salt	5 ml	1 tsp	1 tsp
Sugar	5 ml	1 tsp	1 tsp
Chopped coriander			
(cilantro) leaves	15 ml	1 tbsp	1 tbsp

1. Heat the oil, add the Basic Curry Sauce and cook for 2 minutes.

2. Add the potato, cauliflower, salt, sugar and coriander leaves and heat through for about 3 minutes.

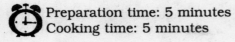 Preparation time: 5 minutes
Cooking time: 5 minutes

ALOO PALAK

Potato and spinach in a creamy sauce. Use whatever tpye of cream you have available.

Serves 2	Metric	Imperial	American
Oil	30 ml	2 tbsp	2 tbsp
Basic Curry Sauce (page 22)	75 ml	5 tbsp	5 tbsp
Frozen spinach, thawed and chopped	100 g	4 oz	1/4 lb
Potato, cooked and halved	225 g	8 oz	1/2 lb
Salt	5 ml	1 tsp	1 tsp
Sugar	5 ml	1 tsp	1 tsp
Cream	15 ml	1 tbsp	1 tbsp

1. Heat the oil, add the Basic Curry Sauce and cook for 2 minutes.

2. Add the spinach and cook for 3 minutes.

3. Add the potato, salt, sugar and cream and heat through gently for about 3 minutes. Do not boil.

Preparation time: 5 minutes
Cooking time: 10 minutes

ALOO CHANNA

Potato and chick peas in a sauce made with any type of cream.

Serves 2	Metric	Imperial	American
Oil	30 ml	2 tbsp	2 tbsp
Basic Curry Sauce			
(page 22)	75 ml	5 tbsp	5 tbsp
Curry paste	5 ml	1 tsp	1 tsp
Large pinch of Tandoori			
Powder (page 19)			
Potato, cooked and			
quartered	175 g	6 oz	6 oz
Canned chick peas			
(garbanzos)	100 g	4 oz	$^2/_3$ cup
Salt	5 ml	1 tsp	1 tsp
Sugar	5 ml	1 tsp	1 tsp
Chopped coriander			
(cilantro) leaves	15 ml	1 tbsp	1 tbsp
Cream	15 ml	1 tbsp	1 tbsp

1. Heat the oil and cook the Basic Curry Sauce, curry paste and tandoori powder for 2 minutes.

2. Add the potato, chick peas, salt, sugar, coriander leaves and cream and heat through for about 3 minutes.

Preparation time: 5 minutes
Cooking time: 5 minutes

BOMBAY POTATOES

Spicy potatoes with fenugreek leaves, carom and tomatoes.

Serves 2	Metric	Imperial	American
Ground coriander (cilantro)	5 ml	1 tsp	1 tsp
Pinch of ground turmeric			
Pinch of chilli powder			
Oil	30 ml	2 tbsp	2 tbsp
Finely chopped onion	100 g	4 oz	1 cup
Pinch of carom (ajowan) seeds			
Dried fenugreek (methe) leaves	5 ml	1 tsp	1 tsp
Tomatoes, finely chopped	2	2	2
Sugar	5 ml	1 tsp	1 tsp
Salt	5 ml	1 tsp	1 tsp
Potato, quartered and boiled	225 g	8 oz	$^1/_2$ lb

1. Mix together the ground spices in a cup with 15 ml/ 1 tbsp of water.

2. Heat the oil and fry (sauté) the onion until golden brown.

3. Add the spice mix from the cup plus the carom seeds and fenugreek leaves and fry for 1 minute.

4. Add the tomatoes, sugar and salt and cook until the tomatoes go mushy.

5. Add 45 ml/3 tbsp of water and the potato and coat well with the sauce. Heat through for about 3-4 minutes.

Preparation time: 5 minutes
Cooking time: 10 minutes

MUSHROOMS IN CURRY SAUCE

Serves 2	Metric	Imperial	American
Oil	30 ml	2 tbsp	2 tbsp
Basic Curry Sauce			
(page 22)	75 ml	5 tbsp	5 tbsp
Sugar	5 ml	1 tsp	1 tsp
Salt	5 ml	1 tsp	1 tsp
Garlic powder	5 ml	1 tsp	1 tsp
Button mushrooms	225 g	8 oz	1 cup
Chopped coriander			
(cilantro) leaves	15 ml	1 tbsp	1 tbsp

1.   Heat the oil and add the Basic Curry Sauce, sugar, salt and garlic powder and cook for 3 minutes.

2.   Add the mushrooms and cook for about 3 minutes. Finally, add the coriander leaves.

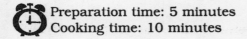 Preparation time: 5 minutes
Cooking time: 10 minutes

BHARE KHUMBI

Deep-fried stuffed mushrooms. Choose a vegetable pâté for a vegetarian version.

Serves 2	Metric	Imperial	American
Button mushrooms, stalks removed	16 approx	16 approx	16 approx
Sheek Kebab (page 36) or Shami Kebab (pages 38 or 39) mix, uncooked, OR any smooth pâté	50 g	2 oz	2 oz
For the batter			
Natural (plain) yoghurt	65 ml	2 ^{1}/2 fl oz	4 ^{1}/2 tbsp
Pinch of mustard powder			
Salt	5 ml	1 tsp	1 tsp
Gram flour	40 g	1 ^{1}/2 oz	1 ^{1}/2 oz
Pinch of chilli powder			
Lemon juice	15 ml	1 tbsp	1 tbsp
Oil for deep frying			

1.   Stuff each of the mushroom cavities with Kebab mix or pâté.

2.   To make the batter, mix all the ingredients together thoroughly except the oil. Leave aside for about 30 minutes.

3.   Heat the oil and when hot dip the stuffed mushrooms into the batter one at a time then deep fry all together until golden.

Preparation time: 10 minutes
Cooking time: 10 minutes

EGG CURRY

Boiled egg in a medium sauce.

Serves 2	Metric	Imperial	American
Hard-boiled (hard-cooked) eggs, shelled	4	4	4
Pinch of ground turmeric			
Pinch of chilli powder			
Ground cumin	5 ml	1 tsp	1 tsp
Ground coriander (cilantro)	5 ml	1 tsp	1 tsp
Garlic powder	5 ml	1 tsp	1 tsp
Oil	30 ml	2 tbsp	2 tbsp
Thinly sliced onion	100 g	4 oz	1 cup
Onion Purée (page 24)	75 ml	5 tbsp	5 tbsp
Sugar	5 ml	1 tsp	1 tsp
Salt	5 ml	1 tsp	1 tsp
Tomato purée (paste)	10 ml	2 tsp	2 tsp
Chopped coriander (cilantro) leaves	15 ml	1 tbsp	1 tbsp

1. Prick the eggs all over with a skewer or knitting needle.

2. Put all the ground spices in a cup with 45 ml/3 tbsp of water.

3. Heat the oil and fry (sauté) the sliced onion until golden brown.

4. Add the spices from the cup and stir-fry for 1 minute.

5. Add the Onion Purée, sugar, salt and tomato purée. Add the eggs and heat through for about 5 minutes. Finally, add the coriander leaves.

 Preparation time: 5 minutes
Cooking time: 10 minutes

OMELETTE CURRY

Omelette in a spiced onion mixture.

Serves 2	Metric	Imperial	American
Garlic powder	5 ml	1 tsp	1 tsp
Pinch of chilli powder			
Pinch of ground turmeric			
Eggs	4	4	4
Salt	5 ml	1 tsp	1 tsp
Butter	15 ml	1 tbsp	1 tbsp
Oil	30 ml	2 tbsp	2 tbsp
Potato, cooked and diced	100 g	4 oz	1/2 cup
Onion Purée (page 24)	75 ml	5 tbsp	5 tbsp
Tomato purée (paste)	5 ml	1 tsp	1 tsp
Tomato, chopped	1	1	1
Sugar	5 ml	1 tsp	1 tsp
Finely chopped coriander (cilantro) leaves	5 ml	1 tsp	1 tsp

1. Put all the ground spices in a cup with 30 ml/2 tbsp of water.

2. Whisk together the eggs, 2.5 ml/^{1}/$_2$ tsp of the salt and 15 ml/1 tbsp of water.

3. Heat the butter in a pan and add the whisked egg. Make a flat omelette in the usual way. Remove from the pan and cut into four triangles.

4. Heat the oil and stir-fry the diced potato until golden. Remove.

5. Add the Onion Purée to the pan along with the tomato purée, chopped tomato, the remaining salt, sugar and spices from the cup. Cook for 3 minutes.

6. Return the potato to the pan, along with the quartered omelette and heat through for about 3 minutes. Sprinkle the coriander leaves on top.

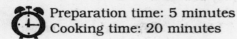 Preparation time: 5 minutes
Cooking time: 20 minutes

INDIAN OMELETTE

Omelette filled with a spicy mixture.

Serves 2	Metric	Imperial	American
For the omelette			
Eggs	4	4	4
Water	15 ml	1 tbsp	1 tbsp
Salt	5 ml	1 tsp	1 tsp
Butter	15 ml	1 tbsp	1 tbsp
For the filling			
Pinch of chilli powder			
Ground coriander (cilantro)	5 ml	1 tsp	1 tsp
Garlic powder	5 ml	1 tsp	1 tsp
Ground cumin	5 ml	1 tsp	1 tsp
Paprika	5 ml	1 tsp	1 tsp
Large pinch of ground turmeric			
Oil	30 ml	2 tbsp	2 tbsp
Finely chopped onion	100 g	4 oz	1 cup
Whole green chilli, chopped	1	1	1
Red (bell) pepper, diced	100 g	4 oz	1 cup
Potato, cooked and diced	175 g	6 oz	³/₄ cup
Salt	5 ml	1 tsp	1 tsp
Sugar	5 ml	1 tsp	1 tsp
Chopped coriander (cilantro) leaves	5 ml	1 tsp	1 tsp
Tomato, sliced	1	1	1

1. Put all the ground spices in a cup with 45 ml/3 tbsp of water.

2. Make the filling first. Heat the oil and fry (sauté) the onion until golden brown, then add the green chilli.

3. Add the spices from the cup and cook for about 3 minutes.

4. Add the diced pepper, potato, salt and sugar and cook for about 5 minutes. Keep to one side.

5. Make the omelette in the usual way, then spread the filling on to one half of the omelette and fold the other half on top.

6. Garnish the top of the omelette with the coriander leaves and tomato.

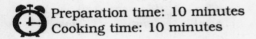 Preparation time: 10 minutes
Cooking time: 10 minutes

CHICK PEA CURRY

Serves 2	Metric	Imperial	American
Ground ginger	*5 ml*	*1 tsp*	*1 tsp*
Garlic powder	*10 ml*	*2 tsp*	*2 tsp*
Ground coriander (cilantro)	*5 ml*	*1 tsp*	*1 tsp*
Pinch of chilli powder			
Pinch of ground turmeric			
Chick peas (garbanzos)	*400 g can*	*14 oz can*	*large can*
Oil	*30 ml*	*2 tbsp*	*2 tbsp*
Curry paste	*10 ml*	*2 tsp*	*2 tsp*
Tomato, finely chopped	*1 large*	*1 large*	*1 large*
Chopped coriander (cilantro) leaves	*15 ml*	*1 tbsp*	*1 tbsp*

1. Put the ground ginger, garlic powder, ground coriander, chilli powder and ground turmeric in a cup and mix together with 15 ml/1 tbsp of water.

2. Drain the chick peas.

3. Heat the oil and add the spices from the cup and the curry paste and stir-fry gently for 1 minute.

4. Add the tomato and 30 ml/2 tbsp of water and cook until soft.

5. Add the chick peas and 75 ml/5 fl oz of water. Bring to the boil, then reduce the heat to low and simmer covered for about 30 minutes. If a lot of liquid remains at the end of the cooking time, increase the heat and boil for a few minutes.

6. Stir in the coriander leaves.

Preparation time: 5 minutes
Cooking time: 40 minutes

Side Dishes

You can add additional dishes from this section to go with your main choice. You will find rice and bread recipes, as well as delicious bhajis, which you can serve with your main course, or as starters with sliced onion and cucumber.

CHAAT

Melon balls with prawns and sauce.

Serves 2	Metric	Imperial	American
Melon	*¹/₂*	*¹/₂*	*¹/₂*
Frozen prawns (shrimp), thawed	*100 g*	*4 oz*	*¹/₄ lb*
For the sauce			
Mayonnaise	*45 ml*	*3 tbsp*	*3 tbsp*
Tomato purée (paste)	*15 ml*	*1 tbsp*	*1 tbsp*
Pinch of chilli powder			
Sugar	*5 ml*	*1 tsp*	*1 tsp*

1.   Make the melon into about 24 balls, using a melon baller.

2.   If you are using raw prawns, cook them in boiling water for about 3 minutes. Drain. There is no need to do anything with cooked prawns.

3.   Mix together the sauce ingredients.

4.   Put the sauce, prawns and melon balls together and mix well. Chill.

5.   Instead of the sauce, you can use Thousand Island dressing.

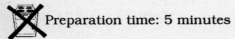 Preparation time: 5 minutes

ONION BHAJI

Deep-fried onion slices in spiced gram flour.

Serves 2	Metric	Imperial	American
Gram flour	75 g	3 oz	$^2/_3$ cup
Chilli powder	5 ml	1 tsp	1 tsp
Large pinch of ground turmeric			
Mustard powder	5 ml	1 tsp	1 tsp
Salt	5 ml	1 tsp	1 tsp
Oil for deep frying			
Onion, halved and thinly sliced	225 g	8 oz	2 cups
Chopped coriander (cilantro) leaves	15 ml	1 tbsp	1 tbsp

1. Beat together the gram flour and enough water (about 75 ml/5 tbsp) to make a stiffish batter. Add the chilli powder, turmeric, mustard and salt and beat thoroughly until smooth. Leave on one side for about 30 minutes.

2. Heat the oil until hot.

3. Put the onions and coriander leaves in the batter and, using your hands, shape portions into roughly shaped balls, about the size of golf balls.

4. Cook them about four at a time in the hot oil over medium heat for about 5 minutes until golden.

 Preparation time: 5 minutes plus resting
Cooking time: 15 minutes

PIAZE

Deep-fried onion bites.

Follow the recipe for Onion Bhaji (page 125) but use very finely grated onion. Drop teaspoonfuls of the mixture into deep fat and fry until golden brown.

Serve with Yoghurt and Mustard Sauce (page 139).

POTATO BHAJI

Deep-fried potato slices in spiced gram flour.

Serves 2	Metric	Imperial	American
Gram flour	*75 g*	*3 oz*	*³/₄ cup*
Chilli powder	*5 ml*	*1 tsp*	*1 tsp*
Large pinch of ground turmeric			
Mustard powder	*5 ml*	*1 tsp*	*1 tsp*
Salt	*5 ml*	*1 tsp*	*1 tsp*
Oil for deep frying			
Chopped coriander (cilantro) leaves	*15 ml*	*1 tbsp*	*1 tbsp*
Potato	*1 large*	*1 large*	*1 large*

1. Peel the potato and cut into slices about 3 mm/¹/₈ in thick

2. Beat together the gram flour and enough water (about 75 ml/5 tbsp) to make a stiffish batter. Add the chilli powder, turmeric, mustard and salt and beat thoroughly until smooth. Leave on one side for about 30 minutes.

3.   Heat the oil until hot. Add the coriander leaves to the batter.

4.   Dip the potato slices in the batter and then deep fry over medium heat until golden and cooked through.

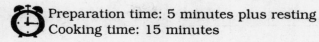 Preparation time: 5 minutes plus resting
Cooking time: 15 minutes

Mushroom Bhaji

Deep-fried mushroom slices with onion in spiced gram flour.

Follow the recipe for Onion Bhaji (page 125) but reduce the onion to 100 g/4 oz/1 cup and add 175 g/6 oz/3 cups of sliced mushrooms at step 3.

DHALL

Lentils cooked with herbs and spices.

Serves 2	Metric	Imperial	American
Garlic powder	10 ml	2 tsp	2 tsp
Ground turmeric	5 ml	1 tsp	1 tsp
Chilli powder	5 ml	1 tsp	1 tsp
Ground coriander (cilantro)	10 ml	2 tsp	2 tsp
Ground cumin	5 ml	1 tsp	1 tsp
Butter OR oil	15 ml	1 tbsp	1 tbsp
Finely chopped onion	225 g	8 oz	2 cups
Red or yellow lentils	175 g	6 oz	1 cup
Water OR stock	900 ml	$1^1/_2$ pt	4 cups
Tomato purée (paste)	15 ml	1 tbsp	1 tbsp
Sugar	5 ml	1 tsp	1 tsp
Salt	5 ml	1 tsp	1 tsp
Finely chopped coriander (cilantro) leaves	30 ml	2 tbsp	2 tbsp

1. Put the ground spices in a cup with 30 ml/2 tbsp of water.

2. Heat the butter or oil and fry (sauté) the onion until golden brown.

3. Add the spices from the cup and fry for 1 minute.

4. Add the lentils. Pour in the water or stock. Stir in the tomato purée and sugar and bring to the boil. Reduce the heat and simmer for about 1 hour (it may take less time) until tender and the liquid has reduced.

5. Finally, add the salt and the coriander leaves.

6. You can speed up the whole process by using canned lentils and just a very little stock, simmering them for about 15 minutes.

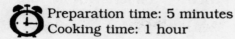 Preparation time: 5 minutes
Cooking time: 1 hour

PLAIN BOILED RICE

Serves 2	Metric	Imperial	American
Basmati rice	100 g	4 oz	½ cup
Salt	5 ml	1 tsp	1 tsp

1. Wash the rice in a sieve until the water runs clear. Soak the washed rice in a saucepan in 250 ml/8 fl oz/ 1 cup of cold water with the salt for about 40 minutes.

2. Place on the heat and bring to the boil. Reduce the heat slightly and continue on reduced boil for about 5 minutes or until all the water has evaporated.

3. Turn off the heat, cover the pan and leave to rest for about 10 minutes.

4. Remove the lid to let the steam escape and fluff up the rice with a fork. The rice can be kept without deteriorating for up to an hour if covered and placed in the oven at 140°C/275°F/gas mark 1.

5. The cooked rice is approximately double the weight of uncooked.

 Preparation time: 5 minutes plus soaking
Cooking time: 20 minutes

Simple Pilau

You will find a recipe for Simple Pilau on page 72.

Karhai Rice

Rice cooked with whole spices.

Follow the recipe for Plain Boiled Rice (opposite) but at step 2 add a pinch of whole cardamom seeds, a 2.5 cm/1 in piece of cinnamon bark, 3 whole cloves, a pinch of ground nutmeg and a small bay leaf.

EGG FRIED RICE

Rice cooked with egg, peas and prawns.

Serves 2	Metric	Imperial	American
Oil	30 ml	2 tbsp	2 tbsp
Thinly sliced onion	100 g	4 oz	1 cup
Prawns (shrimp)	100 g	4 oz	$^{1}/_{4}$ lb
Egg, beaten	1	1	1
Frozen peas, thawed	15 ml	1 tbsp	1 tbsp
Plain Boiled Rice (opposite)	1 recipe	1 recipe	1 recipe

1. Heat 15 ml/1 tbsp of the oil and fry (sauté) the onion until golden brown.

2. Add the prawns and cook for 3 minutes.

3. Add the egg and stir until cooked, then add the peas.

4. Add the remaining oil, then the rice, and stir-fry for about 3 minutes until heated through.

Preparation time: 5 minutes
Cooking time: 5 minutes

NAAN BREAD

Soft bread with egg, yoghurt and milk.

Makes 4	Metric	Imperial	American
Plain (all-purpose) flour	450 g	1 lb	4 cups
Sugar	10 ml	2 tsp	2 tsp
Salt	5 ml	1 tsp	1 tsp
Baking powder	5 ml	1 tsp	1 tsp
Oil	30 ml	2 tbsp	2 tbsp
Easy-blend dried yeast	15 g	$^{1}/_{2}$ oz	$^{1}/_{2}$ oz
Milk	150 ml	$^{1}/_{4}$ pt	$^{2}/_{3}$ cup
Natural (plain) yoghurt	150 ml	$^{1}/_{4}$ pt	$^{2}/_{3}$ cup
Egg, beaten	1	1	1

1.   Sift the flour, sugar, salt and baking powder together.
      Rub in the oil. Add the easy-blend dried yeast.

2.   Warm the milk and yoghurt together then add the
      beaten egg. Pour this mix into the dry ingredients.
      Knead for 5 minutes. Cover and leave in a warm
      place for about 1 hour until it has doubled in size.

3.   Knead the risen dough again for about 1 minute and
      divide into four equal portions. Lightly flour a work
      surface and roll each of the balls out into a triangular
      shape about 18 cm/7 in long by 13 cm/5 in wide.
      The dough should be about 5mm/$^{1}/_{4}$ in thick.

4.   Heat a heavy frying pan (skillet) – do not use non-stick
      – until a tiny drop of water sizzles and evaporates
      almost immediately when dropped in.

5.   Take one naan bread and place it flat on your hand.
      With your other hand carefully coat the entire top
      surface with cold water.

6.   Now place the bread, water-side down, into the hot pan. The bread should stick to the pan. Cook for about 3 minutes over medium heat.

7.   Upend the pan (see diagram overleaf) and hold it over the heat source at an angle of approximately 45° so the heat reaches the bread surface and makes it rise. Cook until the surface is browned and slightly scorched in places.

8.   Remove the bread from the pan with a fish slice. Brush the top with about 5 ml/1 tsp of melted butter and keep the bread warm in the oven, wrapped in foil, while you cook the remaining naans.

9.   Once completely cold, the cooked breads can be wrapped in foil and frozen. To reheat, wrap again in foil and heat in the oven at 180°C/350°F/gas mark 4 for about 5 minutes.

10.   Sprinkle 5 ml/1 tsp of ground almonds on top of the buttered naan bread for a lovely variation.

Preparation time: 10 minutes plus rising
Cooking time: 15 minutes

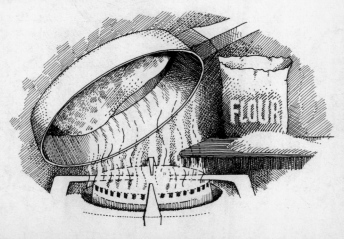

Naan Bread with Caraway

Makes 4	Metric	Imperial	American
Plain flour	225 g	8 oz	2 cups
Sugar	5 ml	1 tsp	1 tsp
Salt	5 ml	1 tsp	1 tsp
Oil	15 ml	1 tbsp	1 tbsp
Easy-blend dried yeast	15 ml	1 tbsp	1 tbsp
Caraway seeds	5 ml	1 tsp	1 tsp
Natural yoghurt	30 ml	2 tbsp	2 tbsp

1. Sift the flour, sugar and salt together. Rub in the oil. Add the easy-blend dried yeast and caraway seeds.

2. Pour in the yoghurt and 85 ml/3 fl oz/5 ¹/₂ tbsp of warm water and knead well for 5 minutes. Cover and leave to prove for 1 hour.

3. Follow the recipe for Naan Bread from step 3.

 Preparation time: 10 minutes plus rising
Cooking time: 15 minutes

Garlic Naan Bread

Follow the recipe for Naan Bread but mix 2.5 ml/¹/₂ tsp of garlic powder with each 5 ml/1 tsp of butter before rubbing on the surface of the cooked bread at step 8.

CHAPATTIS

Makes 4	Metric	Imperial	American
Chapatti flour OR half wholewheat flour and half plain (all-purpose) white flour, mixed together	100 g	4 oz	1 cup
Salt	5 ml	1 tsp	1 tsp

1. Put the flour and salt in a bowl and add enough cold water to mix to a softish dough. Knead for 5 minutes. Cover and leave aside for about an hour.

2. Knead the dough again for 1 minute. Divide into four equal portions and roll each into a ball. Roll out each ball on a lightly floured surface into a thin circle about 15-20 cm/6-8 in across.

3. Heat a 25 cm/10 in frying pan (skillet) until hot. Add a chapatti and cook for about 1-2 minutes over medium heat. Turn over and cook the other side for a further 1-2 minutes. The bread should start to puff up in places (you can help it along by pressing gently with a tea-towel (dish cloth) rolled up into a ball shape). Remove from the pan and store wrapped in foil in a low oven while you cook the remaining chapattis.

 Preparation time: 10 minutes plus rising
Cooking time: 5 minutes

Puri

Follow the recipe for Chapattis but, instead of using a dry frying pan (skillet), grease the pan first and then cook the bread for about 1 minute on each side.

POPADOMS

Ready-to-cook popadoms are available in all good supermarkets. To cook them, heat about 90 ml/6 tbsp of oil in a wide frying pan (skillet) and, when really hot, reduce the heat to medium and place 1 popadom in the hot oil and cook for about 5 seconds. Turn over and cook on the other side for a further 5 seconds. The popadom will puff up and turn golden. Remove from the heat and drain on kitchen paper. As they cool they become crisper, and will stay crisp for 2-3 hours.

Alternatively, you can cook them in the microwave. Microwave on High (600-watt oven) for 30 seconds for the one popadom, adding a further 10 seconds to the microwave time for each extra popadom.

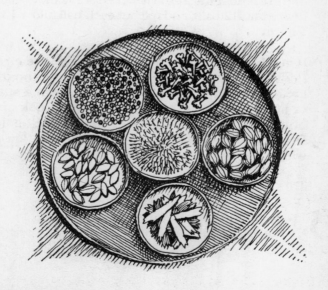

YOGHURT BREAD

Makes 12	Metric	Imperial	American
Plain (all-purpose) flour	225 g	8 oz	2 cups
Baking powder	10 ml	2 tsp	2 tsp
Salt	5 ml	1 tsp	1 tsp
Sugar	5 ml	1 tsp	1 tsp
Egg, beaten	1	1	1
Natural (plain) yoghurt	45 ml	3 tbsp	3 tbsp
Oil for deep frying			

1.   Sieve the flour, baking powder, salt and sugar together in a bowl. Add the egg and yoghurt and mix well (you may need to add a little water). Knead for 5 minutes, cover and leave for 2-3 hours.

2.   Knead the dough again on a floured surface for 1 minute. Divide into 12 balls and roll out each ball into a 13 cm/ 5 in circle.

3.   Heat the oil and when hot add one of the circles. Reduce the heat to medium. Press the top of the bread down into the oil continuously with a spatula or spoon so that it starts to puff up. Cook on the other side for about 20 seconds or until golden. Drain, and keep warm wrapped in foil in a low oven while you cook the remaining circles.

4.   This bread freezes well.

Preparation time: 10 minutes plus rising
Cooking time: 10 minutes

YOGHURT AND MINT SAUCE

Serves 2	Metric	Imperial	American
Natural (plain) yoghurt	*60 ml*	*4 tbsp*	*4 tbsp*
Bottled mint sauce	*5 ml*	*1 tsp*	*1 tsp*
Sugar	*5 ml*	*1 tsp*	*1 tsp*

1. Place the yoghurt in a bowl, then gradually mix in the mint sauce and sugar, tasting and adjusting the flavour to your own taste.

2. Serve with kebabs, samosas or pakoras.

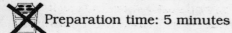 Preparation time: 5 minutes

YOGHURT AND MUSTARD SAUCE

Serves 2	Metric	Imperial	American
Natural (plain) yoghurt	*60 ml*	*4 tbsp*	*4 tbsp*
Mustard powder	*5 ml*	*1 tsp*	*1 tsp*
Sugar	*5 ml*	*1 tsp*	*1 tsp*

1. Place the yoghurt in a bowl. Gradually stir in the mustard and sugar, tasting and adjusting to suit your own taste.

2. Serve with kebabs, samosas or pakoras.

Preparation time: 5 minutes

GINGER AND DATE CHUTNEY

Makes about 225 g/8 oz	Metric	Imperial	American
Dates, finely chopped	50 g	2 oz	1/3 cup
Root ginger, peeled and finely chopped	30 ml	2 tbsp	2 tbsp
Sultanas (golden raisins)	25 g	1 oz	3 tbsp
Brown sugar	75 g	3 oz	3 oz
Salt	5 ml	1 tsp	1 tsp
Pinch of ground cinnamon			
Large pinch of chilli powder			
Lemon juice	5 ml	1 tsp	1 tsp
Mango, peeled and coarsely chopped	75 g	3 oz	1/2 cup
Flaked almonds	15 ml	1 tbsp	1 tbsp

1.   Put all the ingredients in a saucepan and pour on 120 ml/4 fl oz/1/2 cup of water. Simmer gently until the mixture bubbles, then cook on a very low heat for about 30 minutes until it starts to become thick.

2.   Cool and store in clean warmed jars.

Preparation time: 5 minutes
Cooking time: 35 minutes

SIMPLE INDIAN SALAD

The quantities in this salad are really a matter of personal choice.

Onion, finely chopped
Tomato, finely chopped
Cucumber, finely chopped

1.   Mix together. Serve with Yoghurt and Mint Sauce (page 139).

2.   You can use this salad for serving with popadoms.

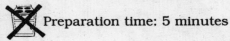 Preparation time: 5 minutes

LEMON SALAD

Make the quantities to suit the number of people you are serving.

Lettuce, chopped
Tomato, sliced
Lemon, sliced
Cucumber, sliced

1.   Mix together. Serve with Yoghurt and Mint Sauce or Yoghurt and Mustard Sauce (both on page 139).

2.   You can use this salad for serving with kebabs and tandoori dishes.

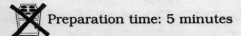 Preparation time: 5 minutes

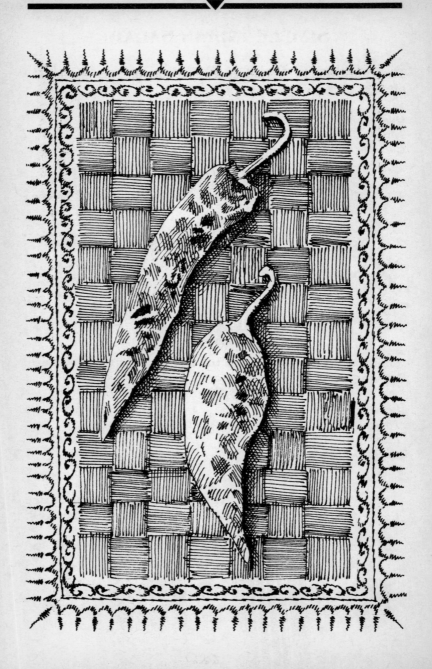

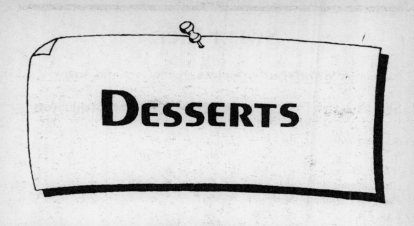

DESSERTS

You may not always want to serve a dessert with your Indian meal, but it is nice to have a selection of recipes from which to choose when you want to treat yourself from time to time.

SWEET RICE

Rice cooked with butter, spices, rosewater and sugar.

Serves 2	Metric	Imperial	American
Basmati rice	175 g	6 oz	3/4 cup
Butter	15 ml	1 tbsp	1 tbsp
Whole cloves	6	6	6
Cardamom pods, seeds only	6	6	6
Piece of cinnamon bark	5 cm	2 in	2 in
Large pinch of yellow food colouring powder			
Sugar	100-175 g	4-6 oz	1/2-3/4 cup
Sultanas (golden raisins)	15 ml	1 tbsp	1 tbsp
Rosewater	15 ml	1 tbsp	1 tbsp
Flaked almonds	15 ml	1 tbsp	1 tbsp

1. Wash the rice and soak in water for 40 minutes. Drain.

2. Heat the butter and fry (sauté) the cloves, cardamom seeds and cinnamon bark for 30 seconds.

3. Add the rice and stir-fry for about 2 minutes until coated with the butter. Pour on 350 ml/12 fl oz/1 1/2 cups of water and the food colouring and bring to the boil. Reduce the heat slightly and simmer for about 5 minutes or until all the water has evaporated.

4. Turn off the heat, cover the pan and leave to rest for about 10 minutes.

5. Add the sugar, sultanas, rosewater and almonds. Cover again and leave off the heat for about 20 minutes.

6. The rice can be eaten warm or completely cold.

Preparation time: 5 minutes plus soaking
Cooking time: 40 minutes

GULAB JAMUN

Deep-fried sponge balls soaked in syrup.

Serves 4	Metric	Imperial	American
Milk powder	100 g	4 oz	1 cup
Plain (all-purpose) flour	25 g	1 oz	1/4 cup
Baking powder	5 ml	1 tsp	1 tsp
Margarine	25 g	1 oz	2 tbsp
Egg, beaten	1	1	1
Milk	5 ml	1 tsp	1 tsp
Oil for deep frying			
For the syrup			
Sugar	200 g	7 oz	scant 1 cup
Whole green cardamoms	2	2	2
Rosewater	30 ml	2 tbsp	2 tbsp

1. To make the sponge balls, place the milk powder, flour and baking powder in a bowl. Rub in the margarine and add the egg and milk. Mix to a soft dough and divide into 16 pieces. Using the palms of your hands, shape into small very smooth balls.

2. Heat the oil until hot, then reduce to medium and deep fry the balls together for about 5 minutes until dark golden brown. Remove from the oil and drain.

3. To make the syrup, boil 750 ml/1 1/4 pts/3 cups of water and the sugar and cardamoms together for 10 minutes. Take off the heat and add the sponge balls. Leave to cool, then add the rosewater.

4. Leave to soak in the syrup for at least 3-4 hours.

Preparation time: 15 minutes
Cooking time: 20 minutes plus soaking

Sweet Samosas with Apple and Nut Filling

Deep-fried filled pastry soaked in syrup.

Serves 2	Metric	Imperial	American
For the filling			
Chopped almonds	15 ml	1 tbsp	1 tbsp
Chopped hazelnuts	15 ml	1 tbsp	1 tbsp
Eating (dessert) apple, grated	1	1	1
Caster (superfine) sugar	10 ml	2 tsp	2 tsp
Pinch of ground cardamom			
Pinch of ground cinnamon			
For the pastry			
Butter	5 ml	1 tsp	1 tsp
Plain (all-purpose) flour	50 g	2 oz	1/2 cup
Hot water	15 ml	1 tbsp	1 tbsp
For the syrup			
Sugar	100 g	4 oz	1/2 cup
Rosewater	15 ml	1 tbsp	1 tbsp

1. Mix together all the filling ingredients.

2. To make the pastry, rub the butter into the flour, then add enough hot water to make a stiffish dough. Leave to stand for 1 hour.

3. To make the syrup, boil 75 ml/5 tbsp of water and the sugar together for about 4 minutes. When cool add the rosewater.

4. Divide the pastry into eight and roll each piece on a lightly floured surface into as thin a circle as possible. (The thinner the pastry the crisper it will be when fried.)

5. Heat a frying pan (skillet) until hot, then place each pastry circle in the pan and cook for no more than 5-10 seconds on each side. Remove from the pan and cut each circle in half.

6. Make a thickish paste in a cup with about 10 ml/2 tsp of flour and 5 ml/1 tsp of water. Take one of the half-circles and brush some flour paste along the straight edge. Now form the half-circle into a cone shape and put in about 2 tsp of the cold filling. Brush the top inside edge with the flour paste and press tightly together. Repeat with the remaining samosas.

7. Deep fry the samosas three at a time for about 4-5 minutes until golden. Make sure the heat is not too high.

8. Drain the samosas then dip in the syrup to coat thoroughly. Remove and allow to go completely cold.

9. Instead of soaking in the syrup, you could dust the filled and deep-fried samosas with icing (confectioners') sugar.

Preparation time: 20 minutes plus standing
Cooking time: 20 minutes

SWEET SAMOSAS WITH SULTANA AND CREAM FILLING

Serves 2	Metric	Imperial	American
Ground almonds	50 g	2 oz	1/2 cup
Sugar	25 g	1 oz	2 tbsp
Double (heavy) cream	30 ml	2 tbsp	2 tbsp
Sultanas (golden raisins), roughly chopped	15 ml	1 tbsp	1 tbsp
Pinch of ground cardamom			
Pastry from Sweet Samosas with Apple and Nut Filling (page 146)	1 recipe	1 recipe	1 recipe
Oil for deep frying			

1.   Mix together all the filling ingredients.

2.   Make the pastry following the recipe on page 146.

3.   Place about 2 tsp of the mixture into the pastry cone and seal well with flour and water paste.

4.   Deep fry, following the recipe above.

Preparation time: 20 minutes
Cooking time: 20 minutes

KIR

Serves 2	Metric	Imperial	American
Butter or Ghee	30 ml	2 tbsp	2 tbsp
Fine vermicelli (seviyan), broken up	100 g	4 oz	1 cup
Milk	600 ml	1 pt	2 1/2 cups
Evaporated milk	120 ml	4 fl oz	1/2 cup
Caster (superfine) sugar	100 g	4 oz	1/2 cup
Sultanas (golden raisins)	15 ml	1 tbsp	1 tbsp
Flaked almonds	30 ml	2 tbsp	2 tbsp

1. Melt the fat and fry (sauté) the vermicelli until golden.

2. Add the milks and sugar and bring to the boil. Reduce the heat and add the sultanas. Simmer for about 12 minutes until it begins to thicken.

3. Pour into serving dishes and serve hot, decorated with the flaked almonds.

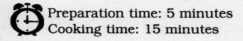 Preparation time: 5 minutes
Cooking time: 15 minutes

RAS MALAI

Creamy spiced cheese balls in syrup.

Serves 4	Metric	Imperial	American
Milk powder	150 g	5 oz	1½ cups
Plain (all-purpose) flour	5 ml	1 tsp	1 tsp
Baking powder	5 ml	1 tsp	1 tsp
Oil	15 ml	1 tbsp	1 tbsp
Natural (plain) yoghurt	15 ml	1 tbsp	1 tbsp
Egg, lightly beaten	1	1	1
For the syrup			
Sugar	100 g	4 oz	½ cup
Whole green cardamoms	2	2	2
Milk	600 ml	1 pt	2½ cups
Rosewater	15 ml	1 tbsp	1 tbsp

1. To make the ras malai, place the milk powder, flour and baking powder in a bowl. Rub in the oil, then add the yoghurt and egg and mix to a soft dough. Divide into 16 pieces. Using the palms of your hands, shape into balls. Flatten slightly.

2. To make the syrup, put 600 ml/1 pt/2½ cups water, the sugar and cardamoms in a pan and bring to the boil. Add the balls, reduce the heat to low and simmer, covered, for 5 minutes. Turn off the heat and leave to go cold.

3. Put the milk and rosewater in a bowl. Carefully take the ras malai out of the syrup and place in the milk along with half the sugar syrup. Chill. Serve the remaining syrup separately.

Preparation time: 5 minutes
Cooking time: 5 minutes plus soaking

MENU SUGGESTIONS

The following suggestions will give you some ideas on delicious combinations of Indian dishes to make up a variety of meals.

Remember that most of the recipes in the book are for two servings, although if you combine a number of dishes you will find the portions fairly generous. Rather than doubling quantities if you are serving more, why not choose one or two more different dishes, and increase the quantity of rice, to make a more intresting meal?

Menu 1

Popadoms (page 137) with Simple Indian Salad (page 141) and Yoghurt and Mint Sauce (page 139)

Sheek Kebab (page 36), Chicken Tikka Masala (page 80), Lamb Rogan Josh (page 51), Aloo Matar (page 110) , Simple Pilau (page 72), Naan Bread (page 132)

Sweet Samosas with Apple and Nut Filling (page 146) or pineapple and cream

Menu 2

Mild Shami Kebab (page 38)

Moglai Chicken (page 107), Palak Gosht (page 94), Aloo Gobi (page 111), Chapattis (page 135), Prawn Pilau (page 74)

Kir (page 149)

Menu 3

Samosas (pages 40-42), Simple Indian Salad (page 141) and Yoghurt and Mint Sauce (page 139)

Tandoori Chicken (page 30), Lamb Tikka Masala (page 81), Aloo Palak (page 112), Plain Boiled Rice (page 130), Chapattis (page 135)

Kir (page 149) or fresh fruit salad

MENU 4

Tandoori King Prawns (page 32)

Buttered Chicken Breast (page 78), Aloo Gobi (page 111), Sweet Samosas with Sultana and Cream Filling (page 148), Karhai Rice (page 131), Lemon Salad (page 141)

Kir (page 149) or ice cream

MENU 5

Lamb Tikka (page 33), Simple Indian Salad (page 141)

Honey Chicken (page 104), Prawn Bhuna (page 57), Simple Pilau (page 72)

Sweet Rice (page 144) or ice cream

MENU 6

Chicken Tikka (page 34)

Sheek Kebab Masala (page 83), Moughal Family Pilau (page 73), Lemon Salad (page 141)

Ras Malai (page 150) or fresh fruit salad

MENU 7

Fish Tikka (page 35)

Chicken Tikka Masala (page 80), Lamb Biryani (page 70),
Mushrooms in Curry Sauce (page 115), Lemon Salad (page
141), Garlic Naan Bread (page 134)

Gulab Jamun (page 145)

MENU 8

Spicy Shami Kebab (page 39)

Tandoori Chicken Masala (page 82), Masala Dosa (page
96), Egg Curry (page 117), Plain Boiled Rice (page 130)

Ras Malai (page 150)

MENU 9

Samosas (pages 40-2)

Special Tandoori Mix (page 79), Karhai Chicken (page 90),
Keema Biryani (page 71), Indian Omelette (page 120)

Sweet Rice (page 144) or pineapple and cream

MENU 10

Vegetable Pakora (page 43)

King Prawn Tandoori Masala (page 83), Karhai Lamb (page 92), Plain Boiled Rice (page 130)

Kir (page 149)

MENU 11

Chicken Pakora (page 44)

Fish Tikka Masala (page 81), Lamb Pasanda (page 87), Karhai Vegetables (page 93), Simple Pilau (page 72)

Sweet Samosas with Sultana and Cream Filling (page 148)

MENU 12

Tandoori King Prawns (page 32)

Chicken Biryani (page 68), Kofta Jalfrezi (page 101), Plain Boiled Rice (page 130), Naan Bread (page 132)

Gulab Jamun (page 155)

MENU 13

Vegtable Samosas (page 42)

Karhai Vegetables (page 93), Aloo Matar (page 110), Mushrooms in Curry Sauce (page 115), Naan Bread (page 132)

Sweet Rice (page 144)

MENU 14

Vegetable Pakora (page 43)

Masala Dosa (page 96), Egg Curry (page 117), Dhall (page 128), Moughal Family Pilau (page 73)

Kir (page 149)

MENU 15

Onion Bhaji (page 125)

Bhare Khumbi with vegetable pâté (page 116), Chick Pea Curry (page 122), Plain Boiled Rice (page 130)

Gulab Jamun (page 145)

Index of Recipe Names